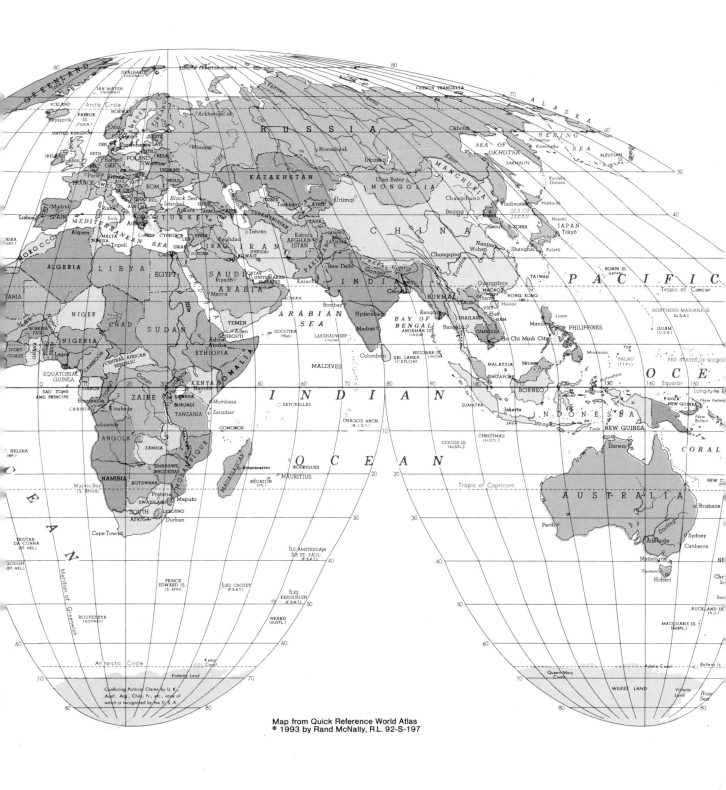

Map from Quick Reference World Atlas
© 1993 by Rand McNally, R.L. 92-S-197

The Borodin Bridge spans the Moskva River in Moscow.

Enchantment of the World

THE COMMONWEALTH OF INDEPENDENT STATES

Russia and the Other Republics

By Abraham Resnick

Consultant: William G. Rosenberg, Ph.D., Professor of History and Chair, The University of Michigan, Ann Arbor, Michigan

Consultant for Reading: Robert L. Hillerich, Ph.D., Visiting Professor, University of South Florida; Consultant, Pinellas County Schools, Florida

Because the Commonwealth of Independent States has no official flag, there is none on the back cover.

CHILDRENS PRESS®

CHICAGO

Women from Novosibirsk, Russia, in traditional costume

For my grandchildren: Daniel, Andres, Gabriel, Alyssa, and Matthew

Library of Congress Cataloging-in-Publication Data

Resnick, Abraham.
    Commonwealth of Independent States / by Abraham Resnick.
        p.   cm. — (Enchantment of the world)
    Includes index.
    Summary: Describes how the Commonwealth of Independent States came about after the collapse of the Soviet Union and introduces the geography, people, and culture of the Commonwealth's republics.
    ISBN 0-516-02613-5
    1. Commonwealth of Independent States—Juvenile literature. [1. Commonwealth of Independent States. 2. Former Soviet republics.] I. Title. II. Series.
DK1.5.R47 1993   92-39801
947.085'4—dc20   CIP
                                                              AC

Picture Acknowledgments
The Bettmann Archive: 20 (left), 97 (3 photos), 99 (left), 102 (center and right); **Novosti Photographs,** 20 (right), 23
© **Virginia R. Grimes:** 43 (2 photos), 54 (right), 96 (right), 118
H. Armstrong Roberts: © **L. S. Williams,** 44 (top); © **Maja Koene,** 67 (right); © **K. F. Scholz,** 87
Impact Visuals: © **Sean Sprague,** 24 (right); © **Jason Eskenazi,** 35, 117, 121 (bottom right); © **Manfred Wirtz,** 106

Photri: Cover, 2, 11, 16 (right), 27, 46, 54 (left), 55 (bottom), 58 (2 photos), 59 (2 photos), 68, 91, 113, 120; © **Zefa,** 32 (bottom left), 36 (left); © **Michail Dmitriyev Novosti,** 42 (bottom); © **AISA,** 44 (bottom), 50, 51, 60, 61, 62, 63 (right); **Russia & Republics Photo Library** © **Mark Wadlow,** 64 (bottom), 65 (left), 86, 101, 103 (left), 121 (top left)
Reuters/Bettmann: 6 (3 photos), 25, 29, 31, 94, 102 (left)
Root Resources: © **Irene E. Hubbell,** 12, 38 (left), 65 (right bottom), 66 (right), 84 (right); © **Jane H. Kriete,** 36 (right), 65 (right top), 103 (right); © **David J. Cross,** 41 (left), 79 (left and bottom right), 83, 111; **Jane P. Downton,** 84 (left)
Bob and Ira Spring: 5, 32 (top left and right), 37 (top), 38 (right), 41 (right), 48, 49 (3 photos), 66 (left), 69, 70 (left), 71 (2 photos), 72 (2 photos), 75, 76 (left), 80, 96 (left), 105, 108, 121 (top right and bottom left)
Tom Stack & Associates: © **Anna E. Zuckerman,** 78; © **J. Lotter,** 82
Tony Stone Worldwide/Chicago: © **Val Kim,** 4; © **Karen Sherlock,** 32 (bottom right), 77 (left), 88 (left); © **Peter Sidebotham,** 37 (bottom left); © **John Lamb,** 37 (bottom right), 42 (top), 119; © **Alan Smith,** 39; © **Barry Lewis,** 40; © **Geoff Johnson,** 77 (right)
SuperStock International, Inc.: © **Thomas Lipton,** Cover inset; © **K. Scholz,** 47, 114; © **S. Fiore,** 56; © **H. Levart,** 88 (right); © **L. Werner,** 115
Top Stock: © **Tony Oswald,** 13 (left), 70 (right), 79 (top right), 81, 110
UPI/Bettmann: 24 (right), 99 (center and right)
Valan: © **John Cancalosi,** 13 (right); © **Fred Bruemmer,** 16 (left), 18, 19, 63 (left), 64 (top), 67 (left), 76 (right), 85; © **M. G. Kingshott,** 52 (2 photos)
Len W. Meents: Maps on 8, 10, 15, 33, 44, 50, 51, 53, 56, 58, 61, 62, 64, 68
Cover: The Borodin Bridge in Moscow
Cover Inset: Produce market, Kiev, Ukraine

Construction work on apartment buildings in Bratsk, Russia

TABLE OF CONTENTS

Communism was toppled literally and figuratively in 1991.
Boris Yeltsin (top), who became president of the
Russian Federation, addressed a pro-democratic
demonstration in Moscow in 1991. Casualties of
the demonstrations were a statue of Felix Dzerzhinsky
(left), founder of the security police, that was
pulled down and a bust of Vladimir Lenin (above), the
founder of the Soviet Union.

Chapter 1

THE END OF THE SOVIET UNION: THE BEGINNING OF THE COMMONWEALTH OF INDEPENDENT STATES

Late in 1991 some of the most surprising events of the twentieth century occurred in Moscow, then the capital of the Union of Soviet Socialist Republics. The Soviet Union, as it was often called, had existed for more than seven decades. It had a Communist system of government. Dissatisfaction, disillusionment, and despair with the way communism was working led to a series of startling changes. On December 26, 1991 it ceased to exist.

A campaign to reform communism led to the Soviet Union's downfall. A new federation of independent republics—united by common interests—was formed in its place. Each republic was allowed its own constitution and government. The federation was named the Commonwealth of Independent States. The first word in Russian is *sodruzhestvo*, which means "community" or "commonwealth," and comes from the Russian word for friend, *drug* (pronounced droog).

■ RUSSIA *Moscow	■ TURKMENISTAN *Ashkhabad
□ KYRGYZSTAN *Bishket	▨ KAZAKHSTAN *Akmola
■ AZERBAIJAN *Baku	▤ MOLDOVA *Kishinev	■ UKRAINE *Kiev	□ TAJIKISTAN *Dashanbe
▨ ARMENIA *Yerevan	▨ BELARUS *Minsk	▨ UZBEKISTAN *Tashkent	

Russia, by reason of its large size, population, and resources, is the dominant force in the Commonwealth. Other members include the Slavic republics of Ukraine, Belarus, and Moldova. Two of the three Transcaucasian republics, Azerbaijan and Armenia, joined the Commonwealth. Georgia, the other Transcaucasian republic, did not join. The five Central Asian republics, those located east of the Caspian Sea, round out the membership. They consist of Kazakhstan, Kyrgyzstan, Uzbekistan, Tajikistan, and Turkmenistan. Three small Baltic region republics, Latvia, Estonia, and Lithuania, had declared themselves totally independent of the Soviet Union prior to its disintegration and have refrained from joining the Commonwealth.

Chapter 2

THE COMMONWEALTH: LAND OF CONTRASTS AND EXTREMES

COMMONWEALTH OF INDEPENDENT STATES

The Commonwealth of Independent States, sometimes referred to as the CIS, is the largest federation of separate republics in the world. It covers almost one-sixth of all the land on earth. The CIS is larger than all of North America. It covers much of Eastern Europe and the whole northern portion of Asia, amounting to 40 percent of that continent. The CIS has more than 100 nationalities, with their own languages and customs, ranging from 145 million Russians down to small ethnic groups. The total population is almost 300 million.

Bordering the CIS are more than a dozen neighboring countries, plus three oceans. The coastlines of the Commonwealth total more than 30,000 miles (48,279 kilometers). Distances by air extend for 6,400 miles (10,230 kilometers), from Murmansk on the Barents Sea in the extreme northwest to Vladivostok in the far southeast. From north to south the land stretches for as much as 3,200 miles

(5,150 kilometers). It takes twelve hours to fly the width of the Commonwealth. A train crossing the CIS passes through eleven time zones and requires one full week of travel.

The CIS can be divided geographically into four main sections: the European Plain, the Ural Mountains, Siberia, and Central Asia.

THE EUROPEAN PLAIN

The mostly flat European Plain is the home of three-fourths of the Commonwealth's people. It is the center of economic life for three of the republics: Russia, Ukraine, and Belarus. The three largest cities—Moscow, St. Petersburg, and Kiev—are located here, along with many other large urban centers. The richest soils, the most productive industrial plants, and thousands of streams and navigable rivers are found on the European Plain. They include the 2,194-mile (3,531-kilometer) Volga River and the winding, meandering "3D" rivers: the Dniester, Dnieper, and Don.

THE URAL MOUNTAINS

The Ural Mountains extend for 1,500 miles (2,414 kilometers), from the Arctic Ocean in the north to near the Aral Sea in the

A forest in the taiga section of eastern Russia

south. Old mapmakers used this range to mark the continental boundary between Europe and Asia. Now geographers often combine the two continents into one landmass, called Eurasia.

The Urals are mainly old mountains worn down by streams and wind erosion. The rounded hills of the Urals have an elevation that ranges from 1,000 to 6,000 feet (305 to 1,829 meters). The Urals are remarkable for the variety and amount of mineral wealth they contain, particularly oil and iron ore.

SIBERIA

Siberia, now part of the Russian republic, consists of three different land forms: the West Siberian Plain, the Central Siberian Plateau, and the East Siberian Uplands. In Siberia, which is larger than the United States and Mexico combined, grow one-fifth of all the trees on earth. The Ob, Yenisei, Lena, and Irtysh, all

The Tien Shan Mountains on the border between Kazakhstan and China

northward-flowing rivers, rank among the twelve largest in the world. Siberia also has the greatest variety of furbearing animals in the world.

The West Siberian Plain lies east of the Urals. Because the terrain is flat, there is frequent flooding. Swamp ponds are common. The marshlands of the region tend to make the plain unsuitable for agricultural use.

The Central Siberian Plateau is located near the middle of the region. The average elevation is 3,000 feet (914 meters). Many kinds of minerals are found here.

The East Siberian Uplands, which extends to the Pacific Ocean, is the largest Siberian region. It has high mountain ranges,

Above: Siberian tigers live near the Chinese border in eastern Siberia. Left: Mutnovskaya Sopka Volcano on the Kamchatka Peninsula

wilderness, and forests where countless kinds of animals roam, including the Siberian tiger, found in the Ussuri Territory near the Chinese border. In the Kamchatka Peninsula there are hot springs, geysers, pink snow, and active volcanoes.

A condition called permafrost, permanently frozen ground, occurs throughout the entire landmass of Siberia. The soil freezes nearly a mile (1.6 kilometers) deep, causing a kind of underground glacier to form. Scientists claim the subterranean ice has probably been in existence since the Ice Age, tens of thousands of years ago. Snowdrifts in Siberia have measured 60 feet (18 meters) high. Rivers freeze to depths of 9 feet (2.7 meters), thick enough to hold the heavy trucks that use them as highways.

CENTRAL ASIA

Central Asia is a low-lying, dry region in the south, mostly desert or semidesert, stretching 1,350 miles (2,173 kilometers), from the Caspian Sea to the Chinese frontier. The principal republics located here are Turkmenistan, Kazakhstan, and Uzbekistan. Some sections are sandy, either black or red, while others are rocky or have hard surfaces of baked clay and salt flats.

In the Central Asian desert belt, usually less than eight inches (twenty centimeters) of rain falls annually. Because the evaporation rate is so high, many rivers dry up before reaching any body of water. Two of the principal deserts of the world are located in Central Asia. They are the Peski Karakumy, or "black sand desert," in southwest Turkmenistan and the Peski Kyzyl Kum in Uzbekistan and Kazakhstan. The considerable fauna of the area include antelope, wolves, wildcats, and various desert rats. Many birds live here in the winter.

THE RANGE OF CLIMATES AND THE VARIETY OF VEGETATION BELTS

Generally the climate and vegetation zones extend east and west across the CIS. The far northern part of Russia is within the Arctic Circle. Several republics in Transcaucasia and Central Asia, on the other hand, are located between thirty-five degrees and forty degrees of latitude. Consequently, the Commonwealth republics have a range of climates from extremely cold to hot deserts and subtropical regions.

Verkhoyansk in northern Siberia has the reputation of being the coldest inhabitable spot on earth. It once recorded a temperature

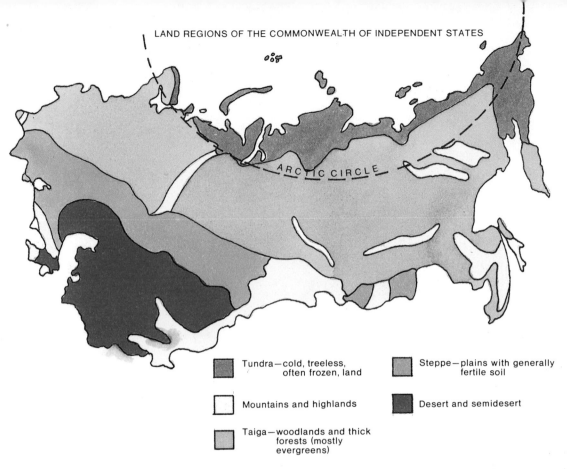

ARCTIC CIRCLE

Tundra—cold, treeless, often frozen, land

Steppe—plains with generally fertile soil

Mountains and highlands

Desert and semidesert

Taiga—woodlands and thick forests (mostly evergreens)

of minus 94 degrees Fahrenheit (minus 69.8 degrees Celsius). The average temperature in January is minus 60 degrees Fahrenheit (minus 51.1 degrees Celsius). In Turkmenistan, the southernmost republic of the Commonwealth, the burning rays of the summer sun can bring temperatures of well over 100 degrees Fahrenheit (37.8 degrees Celsius) for weeks on end.

The variety of world climates found in the various republics of the Commonwealth are factors in determining regional vegetation patterns and, to a large degree, the life-styles of the people. The major feature of the largest republic, Russia, is the extreme cold of winter, except for a few regions in the south of the country. Throughout its history the harsh Russian winter has helped to repel invaders. The winter season lingers for many months, but the relatively short summers can be quite warm.

Trees thin out between the taiga, *which means "woodland," and the tundra (left). The* steppe, *or "plains," is the wheat-growing area of the Commonwealth of Independent States (right).*

ARCTIC AND TUNDRA

A forbidding environment of ice and snow covers the coastline along the Arctic Ocean. In the farthest north, especially in Siberia, a treeless *tundra* prevails. Summers are cool and winters are very cold. Precipitation is light, generally averaging less than six inches (fifteen centimeters) per year. The vegetation in the tundra is primarily assorted grasses, reeds, mosses, and lichens.

TAIGA

The *taiga*, which means "woodland," is a huge east-west band of thick evergreen forest, beginning where the tundra ends. It extends for 5,000 miles (8,047 kilometers) across Europe and all of northern Siberia. A blanket of snow covers the land, in some places 4 feet (1.2 meters) deep, and can stay on the ground eight months of the year. The rivers stay frozen from 70 to 250 days each year. Summers in the taiga can be moderately warm, but soils in the taiga are poor for agriculture.

CONTINENTAL

The climate of Ukraine, Moldova, Belarus, most of European Russia, and the land just east of the Ural Mountains and south of the taiga zone is continental. In this region, which is mainly the European Plain, summers are warm and winters cold. Precipitation falls the year round, but is greater in summer. The total amount of rain and melted snow measures about twenty-five inches (sixty-four centimeters) annually. The vegetation is mixed forest.

STEPPE

Another climate zone is the *steppe*, or "plains." This semiarid narrow strip is predominantly grassland and is situated in southern Ukraine along the Black Sea coast. This zone also exists in an area of Russia just north of the Caucasus Mountains and extends well into Siberia in a strip straddling the fiftieth degree of latitude. Though the rainfall in the steppe is uncertain from year to year and temperatures are variable, it is one of the world's outstanding wheat-growing areas. Crops can be harmed by hot, dry, dusty winds of summer that can bring droughtlike conditions to the region. During the winter strong windstorms blow over the steppe accompanied by driving snow. These high-velocity winds are called *burans*.

Short grasses grow in the desert.

HIGHLANDS

The Transcaucasian republics of Georgia, Azerbaijan, and Armenia are influenced by their highlands and mountainous topography, which give the region a variety of climates. The cold winds from the north are generally blocked by the mountains, but westerly winds can bring nearly 100 inches (254 centimeters) of rainfall a year. The climate is almost tropical in summer, and the winters can be mild, especially in the wide valleys and coastal lowlands. The yearly average rainfall is between 13 and 20 inches (33 to 51 centimeters).

DESERT

In the desert regions of Central Asia where the Commonwealth republics of Kazakhstan, Uzbekistan, and Turkmenistan are located, the driest conditions prevail. The vegetation is short grasses, scrub, or cactus. The summers are warm to hot, but the

The Pamir Mountains in Tajikistan

low humidity makes daytime temperatures bearable. In the desert sands of Turkmenistan, the temperature has been known to rise to about 120 degrees Fahrenheit (48.9 degrees Celsius) in the shade. Nights are generally pleasant. The winters are cold but usually dry and sunny.

MOUNTAINS OF CENTRAL ASIA

The majestic mountains of Central Asia that appear on the landscapes of Kyrgyzstan, Tajikistan, and the eastern part of Kazakhstan carry snow the year round. The CIS republics bordering on Afghanistan and China have the highest elevations in the Commonwealth. Some peaks rise to more than 20,000 feet (6,096 meters). Because the region is so far from the sea and the mountains prevent the lee sides from receiving moist winds, the land is rather dry, considering its height. Winters are cold but spring arrives earlier than in the areas lying farther north. Precipitation in the valleys of the region amounts to less than 24 inches (61 centimeters) a year.

The last tsar to rule in the capitalistic country of Russia was Tsar Nicholas II (left), who was forced to abdicate in 1917 and was later killed. Vladimir Lenin (right) replaced capitalism with communism. Although Lenin died a natural death in 1924, he lived with an assassin's bullet in his neck.

Chapter 3

EVOLUTION OF THE COMMONWEALTH

Before 1917 most of the land that makes up the CIS was called Russia. It had been controlled by a small, capitalistic society composed of *tsars* (emperors), *boyars* (the nobility), and landowners. The majority of the people had few rights or opportunities. In 1917 a successful revolution forced Tsar Nicholas II to abdicate.

Vladimir Lenin, the revolutionary leader, vowed to replace capitalism with communism. He promised "peace, land, and bread" to all who were poor and oppressed. Lenin appealed to the *soviets*, or "councils," who were chosen to govern provinces and regions. His slogan was, "All power to the soviets." A constitution appeared in 1918. Privately owned industries were put under the government's control. Church property was taken by the government. Workers gained the right to an eight-hour day.

A civil war followed. The Communists, called "Reds," fought against the nobility and their army and the landowners, called "Whites." The brutal war lasted for more than three years, but finally the Red Army was victorious.

ESTABLISHMENT OF THE USSR

On December 20, 1922, the first All-Union Congress of the Soviets voted a plan of federation for the four original Soviet Socialist republics: Russia, Belorussia (now Belarus), Ukraine, and Transcaucasia. In the years that followed, additional republics joined the Union of Soviet Socialist Republics (USSR).

The Turkmen and Uzbek republics (now Turkmenistan and Uzbekistan) joined in 1924 and the Tadzhik republic (now Tajikistan) in 1929. Then in the late 1920s Georgia, Armenia, and Azerbaijan entered the USSR. In 1936 the Kazakh and Kirghiz people were given republics (now Kazakhstan and Kyrgyzstan).

The Communists hoped in 1917 that communism would expand to nearby lands, many of which were facing their own domestic crises, but this did not happen. Then, in 1940, Estonia, Latvia, and Lithuania were annexed as republics against their will by Soviet forces. This made a total of fifteen republics. During and after World War II, the Red Army invaded and occupied a number of national territories and made them "captive nations."

Determined to make the USSR all-powerful, the rulers in the Kremlin in Moscow, the capital, resorted to many harsh means to accomplish their objectives.

Weakened by ethnic clashes, famine, unemployment, and frequent changes of government, faltering countries such as Poland, Romania, and Czechoslovakia were taken over by Communists after World War II. Existing governments were toppled by scare tactics, propaganda, spies, secret police, military coups, and activities of local Communist parties. Those who insisted on resisting Communist policies of collectivizing privately owned farms, turning businesses and factories over to

In 1917 people became discouraged because they had to wait in lines at food stores. Shortages that cause customers to wait in long lines still occur.

the state, or eliminating religion were punished or killed. Thousands of dissenters were deported, sent far away to slave labor camps called *gulags*. Soviet citizens who protested were sometimes put in psychiatric hospitals.

Over the years, as the Soviets spread communism throughout the Baltics, Eastern Europe, the Caucasus, and the Central Asian region, Moscow was able to tighten its grip on the fifteen republics. Their governments were run by *apparatchiks*, Communist party bureaucrats who received their appointments through political connections. Corruption, inefficiencies, and the special privileges of these functionaries eventually led to widespread resentment against communism. The people who were once promised "peace, land, and bread" became dissatisfied. Citizens began to realize how unfair the system was.

A shipment of new shoes attracted Moscow shoppers in 1983 (above). In 1991 many shops were empty (above right).

DISENCHANTMENT WITH THE SYSTEM

By the mid-1980s, it became apparent that the Communist system was not working well. Many within the USSR began to have serious doubts that it would ever be successful. Production goals for consumer goods for everyday needs and general use were not being fulfilled. What merchandise was available was often shoddy and limited in supply or variety.

Long lines of Soviet citizens commonly waited outside stores hoping to buy items that were not readily obtainable on a daily basis. Some salable products that were scarce could only be bought with ration coupons. And as the grain harvests declined, food shortages increased. To make matters worse, the system used to store, transport, and distribute food was inefficient and corrupt. Products unavailable in state stores frequently had to be obtained through private vendors or on the black market, where prices were exorbitant. But Communist officials and other privileged people could readily buy what they desired at special shops.

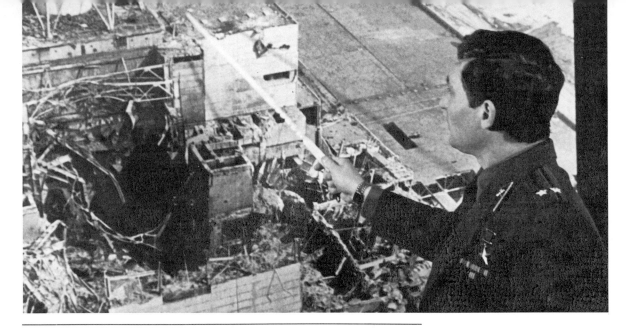

An official points to the fourth reactor at the power station that was damaged in the April 26, 1986 nuclear accident. The reactor later was buried in concrete.

The Soviet economy declined, and the people's standard of living decreased as well. As life became harder it became more difficult to function in Soviet Communist society.

Throughout the land there was a desperate housing shortage. Families were forced to share accommodations with other families. Promises by Communist officials to provide for a better life were not being met.

On December 27, 1979, the USSR became involved in a war in Afghanistan. Soon the Soviet army suffered heavy casualties. It wasn't until April 1988 that the USSR decided to withdraw its troops completely from that region.

In April 1986 a disastrous accident occurred at the Chernobyl nuclear power station in Ukraine. One of the atomic reactors was damaged. About two hundred people died immediately in the explosion that took place. The accident caused a fallout cloud to drift westward over Europe. Thousands living nearby suffered radiation poisoning. Many became terminally ill with cancer. The world community was greatly concerned about the long-term effects on the health of the inhabitants of the region and the impact the radiation would have on agricultural production in the area. As a safety precaution, the power station was gradually closed. Critics cited this incident as an example of how the Soviets worked for the state at the expense of its citizens.

Soviet citizens enjoyed little freedom and few of the fundamental civil rights usually found in other countries. The nation's political, economic, and social activities were governed by a Central Committee and Communist officials from the Kremlin. Large sums of money were spent on building the Soviet military and on nuclear weapons. There was little private ownership, except for small private plots of land held by farm workers. Business, trade, commerce, and transportation were organized around cooperatives or state enterprises. Individuals had few incentives to use their talents or energies. Travel was restricted.

The press and media were censored. The state controlled most cultural, intellectual, and religious expression. All organizations, as well as individuals, were closely watched for violations of government laws and policies. Human rights were not respected. The people had no voice in their government. Active dissent within the USSR against government policies was quickly suppressed by the Soviet authorities. Arrests and sentencing of violators to jails, sometimes without a trial, were commonplace. The KGB, the infamous secret police, caused people to live in fear in what amounted to a harsh police state.

GORBACHEV INTRODUCES REFORMS

In March 1985 Mikhail Gorbachev became the official leader of the Soviet Union when he was elected general secretary of the

Mikhail Gorbachev held posts of general secretary and president of the Soviet Union before the collapse of communism.

Communist party. Knowing that the country could no longer continue in a state of isolation and stagnation and that the people were becoming impatient with the way things were, Gorbachev made some changes. Gorbachev called for economic *perestroika*, "restructuring," of Soviet society and *glasnost*, "openness," in debating issues in public matters. Gorbachev also advocated a "new thinking" in foreign policy regarding international cooperation, peace, and disarmament. Many important old-line leaders and bureaucrats were replaced in an effort to establish new methods of governing. The new social climate tended to do away with restrictions in the media and direct control of the arts was virtually gone. Freedom of religion was to be permissible in a land that had promoted atheism for years.

The most notable reforms included changes in the electoral procedures. The people now were able to vote directly for more than one candidate on secret ballots. Legal opposition to the

Communist party was to be permitted. Human rights activists were released from prison and internal exile. People began to dissent in the press and in public without drastic consequences.

By 1988 an economic crisis gripped the USSR. Street demonstrations and strikes, previously rare in the Soviet Union, now occurred frequently. New laws were passed to permit factory managers and other business leaders to make their own decisions.

Reforms gave citizens the opportunity to own land. Businesses could keep the profits they earned. By 1990 the Soviet Communist Party Central Committee issued policies guaranteeing human rights that were to be protected by a high court. Gorbachev and his supporters began to emphasize the production of consumer goods. Producers did not have to follow set rules. They were free to manufacture, grow, sell, or trade items that were in demand. They could create goods for a new market or provide services wanted by customers. Prices and wages would no longer be set exclusively by the government.

A presidential head of state was instituted, responsible to the National Congress of People's Deputies, the members of the legislature. This body approved Gorbachev as president. A transitional plan was established to rule the country until a new constitution and a new treaty defining relations among the republics and their role in the Soviet Union could be worked out.

The revised structure of government consisted of a State Council made up of leaders of the participating republics. These leaders were elected in democratic elections. The State Council served much like an executive panel. The Supreme Soviet, which was the Parliament—made up of two chambers, the Council of the Republics and the Council of the Union—was responsible for writing and approving laws. A third component was the

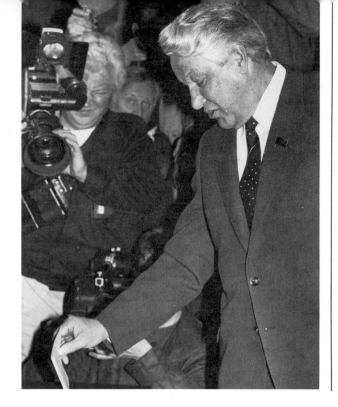

Boris Yeltsin casts his ballot in general elections in Moscow in 1989.

Interrepublican Economic Committee, which was responsible for the economy, economic reform, and social policy. Another important feature of the reforms that were underway was the independence of the courts in decisions.

BORIS YELTSIN, FIRST PRESIDENT OF THE RUSSIAN REPUBLIC

In 1991 Russians elected Boris Yeltsin first president of the Russian republic. He had become the USSR's most popular figure, rivaling Mikhail Gorbachev. For years he had been a faithful Communist official and bureaucrat. Born in rural Russia in 1931, his early childhood years were spent in near poverty. Educated as an engineer, Yeltsin rose to power as party secretary in Sverdlovsk, the USSR's third-largest industrial area.

In 1985 Gorbachev picked Boris Yeltsin to be Communist boss of Moscow. Yeltsin immediately fired dozens of ineffective and corrupt Communist subordinates. Seeing himself as a common man, Yeltsin accumulated very little savings, lived modestly, and refused to accept special privileges. Because he became an outspoken critic of Gorbachev for not bringing about reforms fast enough, Yeltsin was dismissed from his Moscow post and removed from the Politburo. Eventually he was able to win great popularity with the people by blaming the Communists for the USSR's many problems. He then gave up his membership in the party.

Most Russians liked Yeltsin's ideas: to establish a market economy, provide for full property rights, privatize state industry, restructure the KGB, and reduce the size of the country's military forces. Yeltsin also advocated more power to the republics, based on Western ideals of democracy and capitalism. He was elected in a landslide to the National Congress of People's Deputies and named to the Supreme Soviet.

REPUBLICS DECLARE THEIR FREEDOM

By 1991 as the central government in Moscow continued to weaken and as communism began its final collapse after the failure of a coup in August of that year, the Soviet republics were in turmoil. Each of the fifteen republics decided to take affairs into its own hands, virtually ignoring orders from the Kremlin. One by one, they declared their independence.

The three small Baltic republics of Lithuania, Latvia, and Estonia, annexed by the USSR in 1940, proclaimed a full separation from the Soviet Union. By late summer 1991 each was recognized by foreign governments as an independent nation.

The remaining twelve republics agreed to remain in a new

In 1992 President Boris Yeltsin of the Russian Federation met with President George Bush of the United States.

commonwealth, a kind of loose confederation based largely on economic ties. Each republic was to write its own constitution with laws that would take precedence over the laws of the old Soviet Union. The various republics assumed the responsibility of self-determination for all government matters within their respective borders. Georgia, a small republic in the Caucasus, chose not to join the new organization.

By fall 1991 eleven of the fifteen former Soviet republics joined in the founding of the Commonwealth of Independent States. By 1993 two of the original republics left the Commonwealth.

Since the end of World War II, the United States and the USSR had been in a "cold war." They disagreed on many issues, but maintained diplomatic relations. In early 1992 on a visit to the United States, Boris Yeltsin, along with President George Bush, proclaimed a new era of "friendship and partnership," formally ending the cold war after years of rivalry between the two superpowers, the United States and the USSR. Both leaders also discussed further reforms in Russia and the reduction of the number of nuclear warheads deployed by each country.

People from many different cultures—and climates—live
in the Commonwealth of Independent States.

Chapter 4

RUSSIA: THE LARGEST REPUBLIC

The Commonwealth's republics are quite different in size, population, and ethnic composition. Russia is about 550 times greater in area than Armenia and has about 40 times its population. Though the member states retain a large measure of cultural identity, the Russian influence is easily recognizable throughout the Commonwealth of Independent States. This is attributable to the fact that since the days of the Russian Empire and the conquering of their lands by the Soviet Army, they were controlled politically from Moscow. The Russian language, for example, is still prevalent throughout the Commonwealth.

The Russian republic itself spans two continents—Europe and Asia. Its population includes more than ninety different nationalities or ethnic groups. Within the Russian republic, there are specific geographical areas, called *oblasts*, where certain minorities are concentrated. Together, these groups speak eighty different languages. The Russian republic is itself, in fact, a federation of a number of smaller autonomous regions, populated by these different nationalities. About 50 percent of all the people of the Commonwealth of Independent States live in Russia.

THE ECONOMY: PRESENT AND PAST

Russia contributes about 62 percent of the entire Commonwealth's gross national product. At one time, Russia's industrial production was tremendous, with factories producing everything from minute instruments to monstrous icebreakers. The world's biggest hydroelectric power stations were built in the Russian republic. Thousands of miles of pipelines and railways, along with a great river and canal system, transport oil, gas, minerals, timber, and other valuable resources from their places of origin to refineries, mills, and factories all over Russia.

The economy of Russia, along with the rest of the Commonwealth, suffered a severe decline near the end of the twentieth century. Russia has a plentiful supply of natural and human resources. Many people are highly skilled and professionally qualified. Russia is fortunate to have the ability to produce ample agricultural and industrial products.

In Russia and the rest of the republics unemployment—hardly known to the people during the days of communism when a job was guaranteed to all able-bodied citizens—followed the formation of the CIS. Consumer products were often too expensive to purchase. Private markets proved to be extremely high-priced compared to the price-controlled and government-subsidized state stores or cooperatives that existed in the USSR. A pound of cheese could cost a pensioner half a month's income. Chicken, coffee, vodka, sugar, and clothing were, and are, expensive. In early

A man selling odds and ends on a street in Moscow in 1991

January 1992 prices were deregulated. The cost of goods and services was freed. It was thought that in an open market prices would eventually find more realistic levels. Immediately prices shot up to ten times what they had been. Many people's wages, however, remained fixed. More than 60 percent of the people of Moscow were forced into poverty.

MOSCOW

Moscow is located far from the geographic center of Russia, but it is at the center of much that takes place in the Commonwealth. It has been called the heart of Russia, the republic's showcase, Hero City, and the Hub City. The names are appropriate because Moscow is more than the capital of the Russian republic. This eight-hundred-year-old, yet modern, city on the banks of the Moskva River is also the political, industrial, cultural, and transportation center of the country. In Russia, all eyes focus on Moscow. All ears listen to its words. Sooner or later everyone wants to visit here. Many wish to live here as well.

All Russian citizens feel proud of Moscow. It developed like a

Moscow is built on the banks of the Moskva River (right) and Moscow University (above) is one of its high-rise buildings.

huge spiderweb fanning out from the center. The Kremlin, St. Basil's Church, Lenin's Mausoleum in Red Square, and the GUM department store are all in the center.

Most visitors head for the Metro, which can take them underground to just about every part of the city, including the outlying districts. The Russian people consider it one of the world's best subway systems.

Buildings in Moscow extend high above the ground. Besides the many new blocks of high-rise apartments and large hotels, there is the massive Moscow University. The TV tower in Ostankino on the outskirts of Moscow projects like a giant needle one-third of a mile (one-half kilometer) into the air.

Many of the government buildings are located in the Kremlin. Once a fortress, it is now the country's most important monument to its past and present. Behind the once mysterious Kremlin's walls are museums to explore and churches, bell towers, and even a theater. The old buildings on the Kremlin's grounds are architectural models of the past. Their special icons and wall

In Red Square (top), the Kremlin is on the left, Lenin's Tomb is in the center, and the National Museum is on the right. St. Basil's Church (left) was built in the sixteenth century. People in Moscow can get to just about every part of the city using the underground Metro system (above).

*The Bolshoi Theater (above) is
near Red Square in Moscow. The interior
of the GUM department store (left)*

paintings reflect times gone by. But the Kremlin has modern
buildings, too. The Kremlin Palace of Congresses is a marble-and-
glass structure erected in 1961. It was used for special national
assemblies during the Soviet regime and was the seat of the Party
Congresses. It is now used for meetings and theatrical and musical
entertainment. It seats six thousand people.

Just outside the Kremlin wall on Red Square stands the red-
and-black Lenin Mausoleum. Before 1991 people from all over the
world were willing to stand in a seemingly endless line at any
time and in any weather to inch their way into this hallowed
shrine. But now the lines are shorter and more of the visitors tend
to be curiosity seekers. Once inside the tomb they can view the
embalmed remains of Lenin.

At the northeast end of Red Square is busy GUM, Moscow's
largest department store. Like almost everything else, over the
years it too was run by the government. GUM is a two-story
building with a glass roof. It resembles an enclosed bazaar with

Tourists can take a boat trip on the Moskva River.

hundreds of undersized shops that open onto long balconies and a shopping mall below. Now some Western firms are opening their branches there.

There are many museums, art galleries, exhibition halls, and theaters in Moscow. These fine cultural centers are usually housed in magnificent buildings of splendid architecture. But most elegant of all is the Bolshoi Theater. Its gold interior has magnificent chandeliers, a red curtain, and red seats. For those who enjoy ballet or opera, as many Russians do, being part of the audience at a Bolshoi performance is an experience to be remembered for a lifetime. But others seeking entertainment of their choice may want to attend a circus, the children's puppet theater, a rock concert, or a soccer match. Others may prefer to see a motion picture, view splendid church architecture, or even take a motorboat excursion on the river.

During the winter, the Neva River in St. Petersburg is solidly frozen.

ST. PETERSBURG

St. Petersburg was known as Leningrad throughout the Communist era, but was hastily renamed in late summer of 1991. St. Petersburg is the second city in Russia in terms of size and importance. But most Russians think of it as number one, when judged by beauty. Located on the delta of the Neva River, it is built on 101 islands surrounded by smooth rivers and canals. A network of graceful bridges connects the islands. When Tsar Peter the Great founded the city in 1703, he received help in its design from outstanding Italian and French architects. Perhaps that is why St. Petersburg looks more European than Russian.

Today St. Petersburg is the biggest seaport on the Baltic Sea, but because of its northern location, the port waters are frozen four months of the year. Imports must be shipped in during the warmer months when the port is free of ice.

During the early summer, long hours of daylight give St. Petersburg a "white night" effect where dusk and dawn appear to blend together. It is especially noticeable around June 21, when

*St. Petersburg was
designed by Italian
and French architects.
There are elegant,
wide avenues in the
center of the city (left).
The battleship* Aurora *(above)*

the earth is tilted on its axis so that the Northern Hemisphere
leans toward the sun. Of course when the opposite holds true
during late December, prolonged darkness lingers over St.
Petersburg.

St. Petersburg is a kind of living legend, a museum city with
many places that recapture much of Russia's dramatic history. The
cruiser *Aurora*, the naval vessel that signaled the beginning of the
October Revolution in 1917, is moored on the Neva River. The
Peter and Paul Fortress, formerly a tsarist prison, tells much about
the power of the former Russian rulers. And the famous
Admiralty Building, with its golden sailor atop, shows that St.
Petersburg has been influenced by the sea.

At Palace Square stands the majestic pale green-and-white
Winter Palace, now also called the Hermitage. It has been
converted into one of the world's greatest fine arts museums. A
collection of three million items is displayed in four hundred

Above: The Hermitage, which was the winter palace for the tsars, is now a fine arts museum. Below: Many of the buildings in St. Petersburg are brightly painted and electric buses are used for public transportation.

Petrodvorets (left), the summer palace of Peter the Great There are hundreds of fountains (above) on the palace grounds.

rooms. Masterpieces by world-renowned artists adorn its walls. The interior, with its parquet floors and the decorative ceilings of the former palace, is an art show in its own right.

A fast hydrofoil boat ride away from St. Petersburg's port is Petrodvorets, the summer palace of Peter the Great on the Gulf of Finland. Its magnificent buildings, gorgeous gardens, and trick fountains show how little the tsars spared in making their surroundings glorious. After being destroyed by the Germans in World War II, it was completely rebuilt as a monument to Russia's past glories.

However, there is another site that is even more glorious in the minds of Russian citizens than any St. Petersburg palace, church, or building. It is the cemetery memorial to the 500,000 who died during the 900-day siege of the city during World War II. The people of Russia—and the world—will never forget their courage and sacrifice.

Ukraine is called the breadbasket
of the Commonwealth because
its farms yield so many crops
(above). It is also a major producer
of iron ore and steel (right).

Lutsk

L'viv

Kiev

Kharkov

Chernovtsy   UKRAINE   Poltava

Zaporozhye

Yalta

Chapter 5

THE SLAVIC REPUBLICS: UKRAINE, MOLDOVA, AND BELARUS

UKRAINE

Ukraine is a highly developed region in the Commonwealth. The Ukraine republic is situated on a broad plain in the southwest and is about as large as Texas or France. Large parts of the population practice the Orthodox or Roman Catholic religions.

Not only is Ukraine important for its iron ore, coal, heavy industry, and manufacturing, but it also is the breadbasket of the Commonwealth of Independent States. Its warm summer climate and fertile soil help to produce high yields of sugar beets, wheat, and other argricultural products. Many scientific institutes and laboratories are found in the republic.

Ukraine accounts for nearly 3 percent of the Commonwealth's land, has 19 percent of its population, and contributes about 20 percent to the gross national product. After Russia, Ukraine is the leading agricultural and industrial republic in the Commonwealth. Sixty percent of the Commonwealth's coal reserves, iron mines, and some oil are found in Ukraine. It

The port of Yalta on the Black Sea

produces one-fifth of the chemicals and machinery and large amounts of consumer goods.

Ukraine has had a history of territorial wars with neighbors, civil unrest, and internal strife. Polish rule in the 1500s and 1600s exposed Ukraine to European culture. In turn, religious leaders and artists from Ukraine were often able to have contact with the isolated tsars of Russia, and by so doing, supplied them with Western traditions. Warrior-adventurers, called Cossacks, became a powerful force in the region during the 1500s and later served as soldiers for Russia, which dominated the area after 1667. An original union republic, Ukraine became a part of the Soviet Union on December 30, 1922, and a charter member in the United Nations in 1945. Ukraine was expanded during World War II and in 1954, when the Crimea was added. This peninsula, which juts out into the Black Sea, became the subject of a territorial dispute between Russia and Ukraine after they became independent states.

Kiev is on the high green banks of the Dnieper River.

KIEV

The capital of Ukraine, Kiev, is the third-largest city in the Commonwealth. Because it was the ninth-century capital of the first state of the Eastern Slavs, it has been called "the mother of Russian cities." There is an old Russian proverb that says "Moscow is the heart of Russia, St. Petersburg its head, but Kiev is its mother." Now it is the capital of Ukraine and a major transportation, industrial, and cultural center.

Located on the high green banks of the Dnieper, Europe's third-largest river, Kiev is considered to be one of the Commonwealth's most beautiful cities. It has a kind of picture-postcard appearance.

An entrance to a subway station from the main street, Kreshchatik, in Kiev

Upper town, lower town, and downtown areas are connected by a subway and funicular, a kind of cable railway system. Tall poplar and thick chestnut trees grow on the steep hills, in flower-laden parks, and along the broad avenues and cozy little streets of the city. Many of Kiev's buildings were restored after receiving heavy damage during World War II, when the city was occupied by the Germans. They include churches, a famous eleventh-century cathedral, a monastery, and the remains of the ancient city's walls and Golden Gate—all masterpieces of an old culture. For centuries Kiev was the seat of Christianity in Ukraine.

Kharkov, Lutsk, L'viv, Poltava, Uzhgorod, Yalta, and Zaporozhye are important Ukrainian cities. Chernovtsy, founded in the twelfth century, is located in the foothills of the Carpathian Mountains.

Kiev remembers World War II with a flame
that burns at the memorial commemorating
the 100 thousand killed (top) and at
the bombed church of Pechersky
Monastery (above). St. Sophia Cathedral
(left) was built in the eleventh century.

Vineyards in Moldova

MOLDOVA

The Moldovan republic covers 13,000 square miles (33,700 square kilometers). It occupies less than 1 percent of the Commonwealth. Moldova is sandwiched between Ukraine and Romania. Many of its people speak a romance language similar to Romanian or Italian. The region was once ruled by the Turks and conquered by the Romans. The Moldovan people love good food and good music. The food industry always has been a major source of income. The republic produces fine grades of wine, canned fruits, and vegetables. The republic contains nearly one-fourth of the Commonwealth's vineyards. Tobacco and grain growing is important as well.

The capital of Moldova is Kishinev, located in the heart of the republic on the banks of the Byk River.

The majority of Moldovans are Romanians from the Bessarabian region of Romania that was annexed in 1940. Moldova changed from the Cyrillic alphabet, primarily used

50

A residential area of Kishinev, Moldova's capital

throughout the Soviet Union, back to Roman characters in 1989 as an act of defiance and nationalism when it declared independence. In 1993 Moldova withdrew from the Commonwealth when its parliament failed to ratify membership.

BELARUS

Belarus, known as "White Russia," has experienced great changes since World War II. As the westernmost republic, it was on the highway of war for armies pushing eastward toward Moscow and Leningrad (present-day St. Petersburg) in Russia. In Minsk, the large capital city, as well as in smaller towns, the wartime suffering was staggering. Every fourth person in the republic was killed. A large Jewish population that lived in Minsk and the surrounding villages was wiped out. Though the small republic was at one time one of the poorest regions of the European portion of the USSR, rapid growth now is taking place. Minsk has become the center of a thriving machine tool and

51

Public buildings in Minsk, which is the ceremonial capital of the CIS. The town hall is at the top.

motor vehicle manufacturing industry, along with papermaking and building materials. Chemical manufacturing is important. Belarus, like Ukraine, holds a separate membership in the United Nations.

In the south, Belarus has low-lying marshland. Elsewhere, Belarus is hilly and has hardwood forests. Agricultural products include flax, fodder, potatoes, cattle, pigs, sheep, and goats.

Minsk was founded in 1067. Today it is a rebuilt modern city and a major industrial and cultural center. It is considered the ceremonial capital of the Commonwealth of Independent States. The agreement to form the CIS began here, and it is, more or less, the administrative center of the Commonwealth.

Until recently the Belorussians, a Slavic people, had never ruled themselves in modern times. Over the centuries they had been ruled by Kiev, Lithuania, Poland, and Russia, and most recently they were part of the USSR. But Belarus became independent in August 1991.

Chapter 6

THE TRANSCAUCASIAN REPUBLICS: AZERBAIJAN AND ARMENIA

The two Transcaucasian republics of Azerbaijan and Armenia are affected by mountains. They lie in the southern part of the Commonwealth, between the Black and Caspian seas. Historically, this area has been a meeting place for Eastern and Western people as well as a land route for countless invaders of bygone centuries.

AZERBAIJAN

Azerbaijan, located on the western shores of the Caspian Sea, has a varied landscape with lowlands and peaks of the Caucasus Mountains. The republic had been invaded by Arabs, Turks, and Russians since the seventh century. It was conquered by Russia in the early nineteenth century.

Azeris are predominantly Shiite Muslims with historical ties to Iran. The region of Nagorno-Karabakh in Azerbaijan, basically populated by Armenian Christians, has been the scene of violent ethnic fighting and territorial dispute, with hundreds killed since 1988.

The Caspian Sea is to the right of the main square of Baku (above), the capital of Azerbaijan. A group of Azerbaijan musicians (inset)

Baku, the capital of Azerbaijan, has beautiful views of the Caspian Sea. The climate in Baku is dry subtropical, with many days of sunshine. The city, with its shore promenade and green-covered hills, has a most attractive setting, although the area is thick with oil-drilling rigs. The city was founded more than one thousand years ago. In 1901, Baku produced 51 percent of the world's oil. Oil drilling and refineries, as well as an array of other industries, are still important in Baku.

Sheki, another Azerbaijan city, located on the slope of the Caucasian Range, is about twenty-five hundred years old.

Cotton also dominates Azerbaijan's economy. The republic's emblem is marked by an oil derrick and cotton bolls. Much of the machinery used in the Commonwealth's oil processing industry is made here as well. The fruit grown in the region is exceptional.

Fountains in Armenia's capital, Yerevan

Azerbaijan is distinguished for its elderly people. Forty-eight out of every 100,000 residents are over the age of 100. Shirali Mislimov is said to have died in 1973 at the age of 167 years. The average age of the republic's population is 76 years.

ARMENIA

The capital of the Armenian republic is Yerevan, located on the bank of the Razdan River in the Ararat Valley. Yerevan is one of the most ancient cities in the world. It was founded in 782 B.C. Yerevan has its own particular architectural style, with many of its buildings largely pinkish in tone, built of rosa stone from nearby quarries. It is a city of wide streets, numerous parks, and attractive fountains.

Lake Sevan is used to irrigate the southern part of Armenia.

Along with the church being a major influence on Armenian life, the family is another positive influence. Often more than two generations of a family may live together in a household. And along with the family, the spirit of hospitality is important.

Armenians are a social people who enjoy theater, concerts, basketball, and soccer, as well as vacations in the countryside.

The emblem of Armenia shows wheat and grapes, two major agricultural products of the republic. Many kinds of machines, textiles, and chemicals are produced in factories. Most noticeable of all on the Armenian emblem is a picture of Mount Ararat, where some believe Noah's ark may have landed after the Great Flood of biblical times. Now this cherished mountain is part of Turkey, a cause of considerable unhappiness for many Armenians.

Chapter 7

CENTRAL ASIAN REPUBLICS

East of the Caspian Sea lie five fascinating republics: Kazakhstan, Kyrgyzstan, Turkmenistan, Uzbekistan, and Tajikistan. To understand the residents today, it is important to realize that many of their parents or grandparents were horse-riding nomads roaming across the steppe or up and down mountain slopes. One hundred years ago most of the inhabitants of the dry plains and desertlike terrains of Central Asia were herders or oasis farmers.

Until very recently those in power in the Central Asian republics tended to be either Russians or Russian speakers. Even now many have much more in common with Moscow than with Iran and the Islamic roots of the region. But in the hinterlands of these republics, where people speak languages related to Turkish or Persian and where the local mosque is a central meeting place, Islam is becoming increasingly important.

KAZAKHSTAN

Plateau and desert are the main physiographic features of Kazakhstan. Kazakhstan is bigger than any republic except Russia and is about twice the size of Alaska. It extends from the Caspian

An ice rink in Almaty is used for setting speed records (left). A Kazakh man (above)

Sea to China. The Kazakhs are Muslim people of Mongol descent who speak a Turkic language. Many of their ancestors came to the region with the Mongol invasion, led by Genghis Khan. More than one hundred ethnic groups live in the republic now. Only 40 percent of the people are Kazakhs. The rest are Russian, Ukrainian, and Tatars. Kazakhstan plays a significant role in the composition of the Commonwealth.

Largely nomadic, the Kazakhs emerged as a distinct people in the fifteenth century. Since *stan* means "country," the people who live in Kazakhstan live in the "country of the Kazakhs."

Today Kazakhstan has more than twenty-five thousand industrial enterprises. It is one of the Commonwealth's main suppliers of coal. It also produces oil, copper, lead, zinc, tungsten, and other minerals. The Tengiz oil field is one of the largest in the world. In May 1992 an American oil company signed an

*Ascension Cathedral (left), the world's
second tallest wooden building, and
tulips blooming in front of Government
House (above) in Almaty*

agreement with Kazakhstan to help it produce 700,000 barrels a
day over a forty-year period.

One-third of the Commonwealth's wheat is grown in
Kazakhstan. Agriculture, grain growing in particular, is now
possible in Kazakhstan because a canal was built to bring waters
from Siberian rivers into the region.

Situated in the Kazakh republic on the foothills of the Tien
Shan mountain system is Almaty (formerly Alma-Ata), the capital.
The city is relatively new, founded in 1854. A distinctive city
feature is the abundance of orchards, with apple orchards
predominating. (In Kazakh, *Alma-Ata* means "Father of Apples.")
Almaty has a history of earthquakes and devastating rainless
floods from huge mud slides from glacial melting that rush down
mountainsides, depositing debris on the city. In 1994 Parliament
voted to begin phased movement of the capital to Akmola.

Horses are bred in Kyrgyzstan.

KYRGYZSTAN

Kyrgyzstan is a small republic situated along the southern tier of the Commonwealth, sharing the majestic snow-covered Tien Shan Mountains with China. Fifty-two percent of the 4.5 million people are Kirghiz Muslims. The remainder of the population is Russian, Uzbek, Ukrainian, and Tatar.

Bishkek, Kyrgyzstan's capital, was called Frunze until 1991. The city has wide, tree-lined streets and is tucked in the Chu Valley at an altitude of 2,600 feet (792 meters). Bishkek was a mere town of huts until the 1920s, but today it is a modern city with considerable industry. Its agriculture machinery works are most important, followed by meat packing and the manufacture of metalware and textiles.

There are more sunny days in Kyrgyzstan than anywhere else in the Commonwealth. The climate is ideal for growing grapes, cotton, apricots, and tobacco. But since water is scarce in Kyrgyzstan, the breeding of fine-fleeced sheep, pedigreed horses, and yaks is more important than growing crops. Kyrgyzstan ranks

Kyrgyzstan ranks third in the Commonwealth in the production of wool, which comes from these fleecy sheep.

third in the Commonwealth in wool production. The republic is a source of coal and mercury ore.

The Turkic speakers of Kyrgyzstan had no written language prior to 1926. Their literature before the twentieth century was oral, with wandering bards singing tales of past glory to assembled sheepherders.

TURKMENISTAN

Turkmenistan is located east of the Caspian Sea at the southernmost reaches of the Commonwealth. It has a common boundary with Iran. The republic is composed of Turkmen, Russians, Uzbeks, and Kazakhs. The population is predominantly Muslim in religion and culture. Turkmenistan is a land full of contrasts. In the vast reaches of the interior hardly anyone lives for hundreds of miles around.

The republic blends the ancient with the modern. Some people ride on horses, others ride in buses. Some live in tents, others in apartments. Some are weavers of fine handmade carpets, others

Oil has been found in the desert of Turkmenistan.

are technicians in oil and chemical refineries. In some parts excellent cotton can be grown, but in most of Turkmenistan nothing grows.

Ashkhabad is the capital of Turkmenistan. It is located at the junction of the Kopet Mountains and the Peski Karakumy, the hot, dry desert east of the Caspian Sea. The city gets less than four inches (ten centimeters) of rainfall per year. The famous Kara-Kum canal, one of the world's foremost water development projects of the twentieth century, passes near the city.

Eighty percent of Turkmenistan is a notorious moonscape desert, the Peski Karakumy. A brutal sun fries the desert by day, but at night campfires ward off the chill brought on by rapidly falling temperatures.

*A station of the subway system (above)
and newly constructed apartment
buildings (left) in Tashkent*

UZBEKISTAN

About 70 percent of the residents of Uzbekistan are Uzbek
Muslims. Uzbeks form the third-largest nationality in the
Commonwealth.

The capital, Tashkent, is the largest city in the Central Asian
republics. Tashkent is a beautiful city with wide avenues and
ornamental ponds. Tashkent has existed for two thousand years,
but today it is both ancient and modern, Middle Eastern and
Western in architectural style. When the city was destroyed by an
earthquake in 1964, people from all over the Soviet Union joined
in the effort to rebuild it. Many citizens move about by means of
an underground metro system lying beneath what once were
caravan paths of centuries past.

*The ancient city fortress of Bukhara (above)
and Registan Square in Samarkand (below)*

A mosque with a turquoise and gold tiled tower (far left); a bearded, turbaned elder (left); and women in caftans (below) are reflections of the Islamic influence in Uzbekistan.

   Uzbekistan prides itself on having two picturesque cities with Islamic architecture and fascinating bonds to the past. Both Samarkand and Bukhara are richly endowed with mosques, colorful tiled turquoise and gold towers, *madrasahs,* "religious schools," and bazaars with antique allure. Archaeologists have uncovered the ruins of eleven different civilizations that once existed in the region. Young people in contemporary Western attire often can be seen walking past mud huts, twelfth-century minarets, ancient gates, and thousand-year-old tombs. Yet bearded, turbaned elders dressed in dark flowing robes, along with peasant women wearing patterned shawls and caftans, may be viewed riding past newly constructed buildings in donkey-drawn carts.

A fountain in front of the Parliament Building in Tashkent (above) and a vendor selling grapes (inset) in the market

In the snowcapped Tien Shan Mountains of Uzbekistan one can get a suntan in cool air. Miles below in the large, hot, dry capital city of Tashkent, a tourist (of which there are many) may have to stop at one of the numerous and beautifully designed water fountains to cool off. Both Tashkent and Samarkand were once stops along the busy Silk Road from China to Europe. Invaders burned them down time and time again.

The main crop in Uzbekistan is cotton, although the percentage of land devoted to cotton recently has been reduced from 70 percent to 50 percent. Rice and grapes and other fruit are important irrigated farm products. Magnificent skills abound, and the famous astrakhan furs (lambs' fur) are produced in the republic. Uzbekistan produces a wide assortment of minerals and manufactures many kinds of machines and equipment. For many Westerners, its most unusual product is a delicious green tea.

Springtime in the Pamir mountain range (above) and folk musicians (right) of Tajikistan

TAJIKISTAN

Many regard the people of Tajikistan as the most beautiful in the Commonwealth. The young women wear their thick black hair in long braids. They wear brightly colored silks, a vestlike *kemsal*, a skirt, a shawl, and trousers. Men are often garbed in a *chapon*, a black quilted robe. Both men and women wear skullcaps called *tuppis*, a Muslim custom. Shoeless men gather at teahouses and sip sugarless green tea.

Tajikistan is a mountainous country. In the Pamir range, Communism Peak at 24,590 feet (7,495 meters) and Lenin Peak at 23,405 feet (7,134 meters) are the highest mountains in the Commonwealth and rank among the highest in the world. Both peaks have yet to be renamed. The mountains are being explored for coal, oil, gas, and other valuable minerals.

Most of the Tajik population live in the republic's river valleys where cattle and sheep are raised. About six in ten are Tajiks,

A man carrying brooms in the market of Dushanbe

descendants of Iranian people. They still speak a type of Iranian
language. Uzbeks make up 23 percent of the population and
Russians number one in ten.

Large families are common in Tajikistan, and like other Muslim
Central Asian republics, the birth rate is higher than in the rest of
the Commonwealth. Tajikistan is the most conservative and
traditional of all Central Asian republics.

Dushanbe is the capital of Tajikistan, located in the foothills of
the Pamir Mountains. The city was founded in 1924.

In Tajikistan, when the snow on the mountain peaks melts each
spring, the rapid runoff that used to swell the rivers and flood the
fields is controlled by a high dam. The turbulent rivers are put to
good use. Electricity is produced and the water is distributed to
mountain valleys, making fertile the once-barren land. Cotton
along with grapes and other fruit are grown here.

Engineers in the control room of the hydroelectric plant at Bratsk

A VARIETY OF CITIES AND SPECIAL PLACES

In an area as vast as the Commonwealth one can expect to find many different types of cities. From L'viv, an industrial city of Ukraine not far from the Polish border, to Vladivostok, the great naval base and seaport on the Pacific Ocean, hundreds of cities dot the Commonwealth landscape. These cities, like the people who live in them, vary in size, appearance, and personality.

Many Commonwealth cities are situated on the banks of rivers. They received their early starts as trading settlements handling goods moving along the rivers. The Russian city of Volgograd, with its key location on the Volga River, is a good example of this. Founded in 1589, it originally was named Tsaritsyn. Today it is a city that specializes in tractor building and chemical and food industries.

Bratsk, Russia, is situated in the southwest part of the East Siberian Uplands on the lower Angara River. It is a fairly new industrial city developing rapidly in connection with one of the world's largest hydroelectric plants, built here in 1964.

The central square (left) and browsers at a bookstall (right) in Khabarovsk

Irkutsk was founded in 1661 in Russia. Located on the Angara River, it became a frontier for Siberian pioneers. More than half a million people live in Irkutsk now.

Khabarovsk is one of the major cities of Russia in the Far East, located on the bank of the Amur River. Founded in 1858, it is an important station on the Trans-Siberian Railroad.

Krasnoyarsk, Russia, on the Yenisei River in the Central Siberian Plateau, was founded as a fort in 1628. It began to grow only in the nineteenth century with the discovery of gold in the area. It is an industrial center that specializes in aluminum plants and timber processing. The K26 top-secret underground plant that produced plutonium, used for making nuclear weapons, was located near the city.

Rostov-on-the-Don, located on the Don River in the southern area of the European Plains in Russia, is twenty-eight miles (forty-five kilometers) from the Sea of Azov.

The cities of Omsk, Samara (formerly Kuibyshev), and Nizhny Novgorod (formerly Gorky) have populations of more than a

In Russia, reminders of the past can be seen in an old wooden house in Irkutsk (left) and the ancient market churches in Yaroslav courtyard in Nizhny Novgorod (above).

million. Sverdlovsk was renamed Ekaterinburg after Catherine the Great. Novgorod, Pskov, Smolensk, Suzdal, and Yaroslav are ancient Russian cities that date back to the ninth, tenth, and eleventh centuries. Pyatigorsk and Sochi are well-known health and recreation resorts in the Caucasus.

Chelyabinsk was among twenty-one restricted military industrial cities spread around Russia before the collapse of the Soviet Union. The nuclear complex was so secret that Chelyabinsk was never shown on Soviet maps. Some call the area "the most polluted spot on earth" because of the years of contamination from radioactive waste.

LAKE BAIKAL

Lake Baikal, located in the southern part of eastern Siberia, is almost one mile (1.6 kilometers) deep. It extends for 400 miles (644 kilometers) in length and is up to 49 miles (79 kilometers) wide. Its basin contains 20 percent of all the freshwater resources

A farming area on Lake Baikal, the world's deepest freshwater lake (above) and a public beach at Sochi on the Black Sea (inset)

on earth. Lake Baikal contains 80 percent of Russia's freshwater supply. Some 336 rivers and streams empty into the lake. Lake Baikal is the deepest continental lake in the world. It has a great variety of fish. Russian folk songs refer to it as the glorious and sacred sea.

AKADEMGORODOK

Akademgorodok, which means "Small Academic Town," is Siberia's largest city. It is a special national research center. People live and work here in an atmosphere that resembles a well-planned college campus. Life is quite comfortable for Akademgorodok's scientists and technicians and their families.

Chapter 8

LIFE-STYLES OF
THE PEOPLE

Society and class structure in the Commonwealth are undergoing many changes. Before the Revolution of 1917 most of the people were peasants, small farmers, or farm workers. A minority were workers, self-employed shopkeepers, or businesspeople referred to as *bourgeoisie*. During recent times more than 60 percent were classified as workers or industrial-management personnel, 23 percent *intelligentsia* or members of the professions, and 15 percent were collective, or state farm, peasants. When the CIS was formed, a new society developed, one with opportunities for upward social and geographic mobility. Life-styles changed, too, especially for younger people. Yet, historical roots are deep.

During the Soviet regime, the life-styles of the people were controlled by the government in Moscow. Many restrictions were placed on people's independence and their ability to choose their way of life. Their lives also tended to be conditioned by national traditions, their heritage, their occupation, and by geographic factors, including the location of their homes in farm villages, towns, or large cities.

More than one hundred nationalities live in the Commonwealth, the third-largest political organization in the world in population (after China and India). All nationalities have their own carefully preserved history, art, language, and tradition. The language used throughout most of the Commonwealth is Russian, but each republic has its own official language. In all, 130 different languages are spoken.

RELIGION—THEN AND NOW

During the Soviet era organized religion was frowned on. The policy of the government was antireligious, even though the Soviet constitution "guaranteed" freedom of religious worship. Atheism was encouraged and promoted, especially for the younger generation. Religious beliefs were considered superstitions held by backward or narrow-minded people. For those who were believers or who were seen going to a church, mosque, or synagogue, there was often ridicule, lost opportunities for a higher education, or little chance for a job promotion. It was estimated that 20 percent of the population, mostly older persons, were somewhat observant.

Religion was practiced privately, either in the home or in officially recognized functioning churches. Few seminaries were allowed to exist and many former houses of worship were turned into museums, warehouses, or social clubs. Religious instruction was not permitted in public schools, and parochial "Sunday" schools were not allowed.

When Mikhail Gorbachev proclaimed his glasnost policy for the USSR in the 1980s, a religious reawakening occurred. People old and young either returned to religion or were exposed to it for the first time.

Now there are forty religious denominations in the Commonwealth. More than twenty thousand Russian Orthodox,

The Church of the Transfiguration near St. Petersburg is built entirely of wood.

Catholic, Lutheran, and Old Believers' churches, Jewish synagogues, Muslim mosques, Buddhist temples, and meeting houses of other faiths are operating throughout the Commonwealth. Seminaries and religious academies are once again becoming important religious education centers.

Russian Orthodox is the main religion in the Commonwealth. About 200 million people support this offshoot of the the Eastern Orthodox branch of Christianity on the basis of their parental or ancestral heritage. Western Christian religions, both Roman Catholic and Protestant, account for 2 percent of religious affiliation in the republics. The Armenian church has 1.5 percent of those who follow Christianity. Muslims make up 21 percent and Buddhists and others total less than 0.5 percent of the religious population. Before and during the Communist years, the Jewish population was as high as 1 percent. Jews in the USSR suffered prejudice and persecution. In the 1970s and 1980s hundreds of thousands were permitted to emigrate to the United States and Israel.

Above: The ornate facade of the Registan in Samarkand   Left: The interior of St. Sophia Cathedral in Nizhny Novgorod, built in the eleventh century

The people of the Commonwealth are extremely proud of their religious buildings. Many reflect extraordinary centuries-old architecture patterned after Byzantine masterpieces. There are splendid frescoes, icons, ornate wall coverings, and altar screens. The mosques of Central Asia, with their old walls, blue domes, arches, and geometric ornamentations, are strikingly attractive. There is a colorful Siberian Buddhist temple in Ulan-Ude, Russia. Synagogues, designed with balconies separating women congregants from men during prayer services, are now opening in almost every major city in the Commonwealth.

THE ROLE OF WOMEN

Both parents in a family usually work. More women than men hold jobs, and they do almost any kind of work except mining. Seventy-five percent of the doctors are women. Many women are

Women in St. Petersburg (left) are dressed for the winter weather.
In Bukhara, women work at an embroidery factory (right).

engineers and scientists. Besides working, women are usually responsible for shopping, which often includes time standing in line waiting to be served.

For a female born in Central Asia—even today—there is a likelihood that her husband will be selected by her mother. In remote places there may still be a bride price paid on her behalf. At age nine or ten she must prepare for her marriage, which will likely take place before her sixteenth birthday. A religious divorce can be obtained readily by Central Asian men, but almost never by a woman in this part of the Commonwealth. A woman's mother-in-law constantly supervises the marriage. Because their families tend to be quite large, much of the daily routine of Central Asian women is directed toward home care and child rearing.

Generally, the status of women in the Muslim republics is below that of men. However, that is beginning to change in the more urban areas of Central Asia. Many work on farms and in industrial enterprises.

Ukrainian babushkas in the typically decorated interior of a rural home

In Russia and the Slavic republics, the grandmother plays a significant role in the family. Grandmothers, endearingly called *babushkas*, are credited with holding society together. (In Western countries a babushka is a popular kerchief or scarf worn on the head.) Babushkas are usually retired, and because they have such meager pensions, many are forced to live in cramped quarters with their children. They shop, which may take a good part of the day, clean the house, do the laundry, cook, and take care of the grandchildren. In that way, they free other members of the family to pursue other activities.,

Russian grandmothers often work to supplement their income by doing underpaid menial jobs, such as shoveling snow, cleaning streets, washing floors, or acting as attendants in clinics and hospitals.

Much of the fresh food served at this Siberian farm table (far left) comes from the farm. Caviar and cheese on bread (above) is a famous Russian hors d'oeuvre. This woman (left) is turning cucumbers into dill pickles.

FOOD

What is eaten in the Commonwealth depends on nationality and availability. Because of shortages, the people's diet is usually low on meat and dairy products. When available, meat is expensive. In the wintertime fresh vegetables and fruit are not plentiful. People rely on bread, starches, sausages, canned fish, cabbage, and beets in preparing their meals.

In the Slavic republics, cabbage and potatoes are staple food items. *Borscht*, a soup made with beets, and *kasha*, a cereal grain, are favorites in the Russian diet. So is sour cream. It seems that no meal is complete without freshly baked bread.

Moldovan cuisine includes mutton dishes; *brynza*, "cheese"; *mamalyga*, a porridge made of barley; and chestnut meal or corn meal.

Chunks of lamb are cooked on a grill in a market in Uzbekistan.

In the Transcaucasian republics the food is often similar to dishes from Turkey and Greece. Lamb pieces, *shashlyk*, "kebabs," and sausages on skewers cooked over an open fire are a delight for many. A variety of chicken and fish dishes cooked on the spit and topped with melted cheese or nuts also are served. A flat, unleavened, crusty pita-type bread, which is filled with assorted vegetables, is popular. Rice pilaf, local goat cheeses, olives, and fruits, especially grapes, are mainstay foods.

In Siberia, where canned fish, horse, and reindeer are eaten, there also may be some Oriental-style flavorings and side dishes to satisfy native tastes. In Central Asia, *plov*, a mutton and rice mixture, is popular.

The teapot or family *samovar*, the ever-present Russian urn for making tea, supplies the beverage for the meal. Tea in Russia is called *chai*, which refers to its place of origin, China. Vodka is in great demand. Wine is also found in some homes.

Folk art and other handicrafts for sale at an art gallery

CRAFTS AND FOLK ART

Throughout the Commonwealth many village people specialize in making craft items and folk art. In Russia small hand-painted, lacquered boxes have become world famous. Equally well known are the *matrioshka*, Russian nesting dolls. Other handicrafts include intricate woodwork, bone carvings, woolen kerchiefs, delicate porcelain figures, and colorful embroidery.

Traditional hand-painted Easter eggs from Ukraine

In rural Belarus women spin flax to make linen for household articles and clothing. Metal casting and stamping from the Caucasus is much in demand. Azerbaijanis make gold-threaded shawls and gem-studded belts. Tajik craftspeople fashion decorative skullcaps, tablecloths, and wood carvings. For centuries the Kirghiz have been making and playing the *kamuz*, a three-stringed musical instrument.

HOMES

In the Commonwealth it is most likely that a person will reside in one of the millions of apartments in the labyrinth of mid and high-rise uniform buildings constructed in every city. Rural dwellers often live in old weather-beaten farmhouses with wells and outbuildings. Others might live in log houses, wood cottages with steep tin roofs, stucco-covered stone buildings, or even *yurts*,

A school has been built in the center of this apartment complex in St. Petersburg.

circular tents made of felt or skins on a framework of poles that are used by nomadic herders.

During World War II more than six million homes throughout Russia were destroyed. That was almost half of the housing. In rebuilding the country new industries were started all over the land. New cities sprang up rapidly. Housing was needed immediately for the workers. Millions of apartments were constructed, but there is still a serious housing shortage in the Commonwealth.

Most of the single-family homes that remain in the cities are used to their fullest until new apartments are ready. Sometimes they house more than one family. Each family may be required to share a kitchen and bathroom.

In the villages, especially in Russia, the homes are constructed of wood or logs taken from nearby forests. The windows of village homes often are decorated. They are enclosed by hand-carved

A house in Irkutsk (inset) has a decorative window brightened with flowers. In Bratsk (above), the shutters and the picket fence of this house have been painted blue.

frames, usually painted blue. Inside the homes, bright printed fabrics are used for tablecloths and window curtains. The furnishings are usually simple but functional. A sofa often serves as a bed. Sometimes sleeping cots are placed in the kitchen. Balconies are used for storage. An icon, appreciated more for its art than for its religious significance, may hang from the living room wall.

In the southern republics, decorative rugs adorn the walls. Small fenced-in backyard gardens of these country homes contain vegetables, grapevines, and sunflowers. Nearby a cow may be grazing next to the family-owned chickens, geese, and ducks.

Russian villages tend to be clusters of houses, barns, and sheds closely connected to each other by wood fences and backyard paths. They often straddle a dirt or gravel road that leads to another village. Deep winter snows and the soft, gluelike mud of spring can turn a village into a temporary prison for six months of the year.

Teenagers on a Moskva River cruise boat

YOUTH ACTIVITIES

The Commonwealth republics have a history of highly organized youth activities. In the Soviet Union young people were encouraged to join the Komsomol, an organization of teenagers and young adults. Children ten to fifteen years old belonged to the Young Pioneers. Both groups were indoctrinated into the ideological and patriotic aspects of communism through state-sponsored clubs, camps, sports, and special events. Now similar youth activities are under the independent administration of local authorities, schools, factory enterprises, and cooperative farms.

Under their newfound freedom, the young people of the former Soviet Union tend to prefer activities of their own choosing rather than regimented programs planned by others. They seem to enjoy congregating at pedestrian malls, parks, coffee shops, and youth centers. They play or listen to loud Western rock music and

Chess is played by people of all ages throughout the Commonwealth.

discuss and display the latest fads in clothing, hairstyles, and jewelry. Discotheques, or nightclubs, are popular.

The law generally bars children under age sixteen from working, so there is ample time to see motion pictures, attend concerts, indulge in a hobby, visit with friends, or start a game of basketball, ice hockey, or soccer, more commonly called football. Many girls participate in dance or take ballet lessons. Chess playing is almost universal in this part of the world. It is a traditional pastime for Russians of all ages.

EDUCATION

Over the years, Soviet education was fairly uniform and highly structured. Attempts were made to have all students learn the same things at the same time. Presently there is less rigidity. School administrators can now adjust and customize curriculum for local or regional needs. Textbooks may be written in as many

A nursery school in Siberia

as fifty-two different languages. Even the rule for wearing uniforms has been relaxed. Throughout the Commonwealth there is a wide difference in the conditions and facilities found in school buildings.

Education in the republics is compulsory. Formal education begins for everyone at age six and usually continues until age seventeen. Most children attend preschools, beginning at three years of age, especially if they have working parents and no babushka to look after them. More than likely they attend a nursery run by a factory, enterprise, or trade union.

Schools, especially in Russia, are demanding of the student's time and energy. Children attend class six days a week and receive six more weeks of instruction than their American counterparts. Split sessions are common in many schools. Students usually report early or remain late for homework supervision. There is close communication between teachers and parents through weekly progress reports sent home for parental information.

In St. Petersburg, a youngster wears a uniform to school (right) and a teacher works with a ballet student at the Vaganov Institute (far right).

The courses of study throughout the Commonwealth are generally quite similar, except that the various republics include studies about their national or regional customs and heritage. Non-Russian people have the right to have their children taught in their native tongue. The required courses of study run through the tenth grade. Soviet children are not pampered in school. Much is expected of them. Schoolwork is difficult and is to be taken seriously.

In Siberia, where distances from home to school are often great, correspondence courses are common.

Commonwealth schools tend to have an average class size of twenty-five or more. Instruction for the most part is teacher-directed and rather formal, with little opportunity for casual recitation. Discipline is strict. Teachers are respected and honored. Children spend a lot of time writing notes and answers in copybooks. Commonwealth schools lack supplies and equipment, especially computers and copiers. Many have no plumbing, and some have no running water.

Language studies are stressed in grades one through five and beyond. Literature classes start at grade four. From first grade through eighth grade there are six classes of mathematics per week, then five classes are offered in grades nine and ten. Nature study begins early, while geography is emphasized in the middle grades. Students study biology in grades five through ten, physics in grades six through ten, and chemistry in grades seven through ten. There is a sequence of six years of studying a foreign language, beginning in the fifth grade. Art, music, physical education, and home economics are important subjects. Elective courses start at grade seven. Most extracurricular activities meet after school hours.

SPECIALIZED SCHOOLS

In Russia and the other republics, the system recognizes the need for many kinds of specialized schools. Children with outstanding skills, abilities, or talents are identified early. They are encouraged to attend a special school. These schools might stress foreign language training, military cadet training, ballet, sports and gymnastics, music, certain technical and vocational courses, or even circus and theater arts. But no matter what type of school Commonwealth students attend, they must take a national examination at the end of the eighth grade. The scores they receive could, more than anything else, determine the level and kind of high school they will be able to enter. The best schools, which prepare students for university and, eventually, professional studies, require the highest grades. Lower-scoring students go on to technical or vocational high schools and find work in factories, stores, or on farms. There are about sixty-five hundred vocational schools in the Commonwealth. Many provide instruction in a trade and complete the students' secondary education.

HOLIDAYS

Holidays in the Commonwealth are occasions for family celebrations. They tend to blend old folk practices with newer traditions and festivities. In the Slavic or Christian republics, Christmas and Easter are widely celebrated. Believers and nonbelievers go to the churches for the beauty of the rites and to listen to choirs.

At Christmastime carols are sung and trees are decorated with toys, fruit, paper chains, and electric lights. Gifts are exchanged. The *kolach*, a braided Christmas bread with a candle on it, is set on the holiday table. Twelve meatless dishes are served before midnight mass. Children are expected to look for the first star of the evening, the Christmas star, before going to bed.

People mark the New Year by decorating trees and exchanging gifts. The holiday spirit lasts through the first two weeks in January. The children are particularly happy, for this is the holiday when a red-clad Grandfather Frost, a kind of first cousin to Santa Claus, pays a visit. With his assistant, the Snow Maiden, he puts toys and gifts around the tree on New Year's Day.

Easter, an important observance, continues with traditional customs. Families visit cemeteries, gather in churchyards at midnight, light candles, and sing religious songs. Easter cakes are blessed by the local priest. Children paint colorful designs on eggs for the Easter feast.

Many other holidays are celebrated in a variety of ways in the Commonwealth. On March 8, Women's Day, women are given flowers and gifts to show love, respect, and appreciation by friends and family. The observance of May Day on May 1 honors the worker as well as the arrival of spring. Celebrants participate

May Day celebrations once glorified the Communist party, but are now used to honor the worker and the arrival of spring.

in street singing and watch fireworks displays. Victory Day, May 9, commemorates the end of fighting in World War II. Flowers are laid around war memorial monuments, and a minute of silence is observed.

Shrovetide, the holiday welcoming spring, occurs seven weeks before Easter and lasts seven days. People in Russia believe that the number seven brings good fortune during Shrovetide. That is why so many couples marry during this seven-day period. Shrovetide activities include noise making, teasing, playing tricks, sledding, and snowball fighting. Towns take on a carnival atmosphere with villagers wearing costumes and masks. Pancakes are eaten throughout the festivities.

The different nationalities and minorities in the Commonwealth tend to retain many of their special skills, traits, and customs. They have managed to retain their traditional dances, costumes, and folk music traditions, which they proudly demonstrate at festivals, weddings, parties, and holiday celebrations.

A fascinating ethnic holiday is the Tatar Festival of the Plow. It takes place on June 25. The Tatars ruled Russia during the Middle Ages. This day was set aside to celebrate the end of their spring farming.

On September 1, on the first day of school, children in the republics bring their teachers bouquets of flowers.

September 12 is Mushroom Harvest Day. Mushroom picking is a family activity in wooded areas of the republics. In Belarus, families get up early and take their baskets to the forests, pick only edible mushrooms, and after a day's outing, return home to make pickled relish for the winter.

Poetry recitals are popular in the Commonwealth. Poetry Day is celebrated in December of each year.

Commonwealth people use holidays to attend festivals, sports and entertainment events, go hiking and camping, visit spas and resorts, spend leisure hours in the park, or merely promenade along favorite walkways. Traditionally, families gather at home at holiday time, with hosts and guests providing generous amounts of festive food and drink.

SPORTS AND RECREATION

Conventional sports such as soccer, basketball, swimming, volleyball, tennis, and track and field are popular. The winter season brings opportunities to ski, ice fish, skate, and hunt. Ice hockey is a favorite for boys and young men. Russians excel at wrestling and gymnastics. Recently, visiting American teams have introduced the sports of baseball and football to enthusiastic club players. In the northernmost latitudes reindeer and dog team races receive much attention.

The most popular sport in Ukraine is soccer. For many years soccer teams from the republic won national championships in the former Soviet Union. In Kazakhstan competitive games on horseback draw large numbers of participants and spectators. In one game the horseback riders must pick up a coin lying on the ground while riding at full gallop. Mountain climbing, boxing, and field hockey have special appeal for athletes in Kazakhstan.

Azerbaijanis display exceptional skills in wrestling, judo, and field hockey. Equestrian sports are the most popular in Kyrgyzstan. Riders hunt for small game on horseback using birds of prey. Others resort to golden eagles to hunt wolves. Both are ancient and revered sports in Central Asia. Tajiks are good archers, fencers, and chess players. Wrestling events are well attended in Tajikistan. Boxing, soccer, weight lifting, and track events appeal to the youth of Armenia. Their national athletes have set records in Europe and have won national championships in the former USSR. Horseback riding is a sport that most people in Turkmenistan do most skillfully.

Young people in the Commonwealth are active in competitive sports. Boys and girls between nine and fourteen with outstanding athletic abilities can enroll in one of fifty-five hundred specialized junior sports schools. With few exceptions, most of the sports stars come from such schools. Periodically, nationwide olympiads are held for schoolchildren within the republics. The athletic competition involves participation in twenty-five different sports. The winners often go on to compete in international events, including the Olympics.

In the 1992 Winter Olympics in Albertville, France, 138 athletes from Russia, Ukraine, Belarus, Uzbekistan, and Kazakhstan called themselves the Unified Team. They found a way to mark their

In the 1992 winter Olympics, the CIS hockey team won the gold medal.

nationalities by carrying a small flag from their homeland and wore a matching shoulder patch, a touch of independence reflecting the disintegration of the Soviet Union. Medals were awarded to their winning athletes under the official Olympic banner. When the Unified ice hockey team won their gold medals, the Olympic anthem was played instead of the official song of the former USSR. During the 1992 summer Olympics at Barcelona, Spain, the athletes of the former Soviet Union participated again as the Unified Team, probably for the last time. They won 87 medals: 35 gold, 29 silver, and 23 bronze.

Chapter 9

LITERATURE, MUSIC,
AND THE ARTS

CULTURE IN THE COMMONWEALTH

Culture throughout much of the Commonwealth has rich and
ancient traditions. The literature and arts of Armenia and the
people of Central Asia were developed even in ancient and
biblical times. Russian authors—novelists, playwrights, and
poets—are greatly admired and respected to this day. The many
talents of Russians, particularly in the creative arts, have enriched
the lives of millions worldwide. Notable achievements have been
made in music, opera, classical ballet, dance, fine arts, theater, and
filmmaking. During the Soviet era the government relied on the
cultural arts to advance the goals of communism by subsidizing
and controlling all artistic activities.

Outstanding cultural opportunities are offered in each of the
republics. It is not unusual for native orchestras, ensembles, or
folk dance groups to entertain audiences in other republics and
distant lands. Their performances often reflect the music,
instruments, and colorful costumes of their local origins.

Folk dancers from Khabarovsk, Russia (above),
and Azerbaijan (right)

Especially remarkable are the hundreds of different folk dances that are performed throughout the Commonwealth. Most popular are those that feature four-couple square dances, toe dancing, and those that include spectacular high leaps by the male dancers. These acrobatic maneuvers characterize the dances of the Caucasus and Ukraine.

Scores of publishing houses print books and articles written by regional authors in the national languages of the republics. Libraries, well stocked with books about native heritages, are located in villages and cities alike. Professional theaters, opera houses, and ballet halls are everywhere. Thousands of theme museums are visited by millions of Commonwealth viewers each year.

LITERATURE

The people of the Commonwealth are heirs to a great literary tradition and reputation. Russian literature became a social force

Three famous classical Russian authors are (left to right) Nikolai Gogol, Aleksandr Pushkin, and Fyodor Dostoyevsky.

in the nineteenth century. This period was called the Golden Age, in which Russian musicians, artists, and writers won the admiration of the entire world. Under the genius of Aleksandr Pushkin, the country's greatest lyric poet, and Mikhail Lermentov, romantic poet and novelist, criticism of the existing political and social order came about. They saw tragedy when the aristocracy of that time suppressed talent and creativity of the lower classes. Nikolai Gogol called for reform of the system in his novel, *Dead Souls*, when he exposed the unpleasant side of Russian provincial life. In Gogol's *Inspector General*, believed to be one of Russia's greatest plays, he pokes fun at corrupt government officials.

In the middle and late 1800s, a number of outstanding Russian literary figures influenced the minds of the nation's readers. Ivan Turgenev portrayed rural life. Leo Tolstoy reported on many characters and social customs of his time in his heroic novels, *War and Peace* and *Anna Karenina*. Fyodor Dostoyevsky, in *Crime and Punishment* and *The Brothers Karamazov*, selected the theme of the need of religious faith to offset the negative behaviors of city life.

Anton Chekhov wrote stories and sensitive dramas about hopelessness, despair, and isolation of the declining nobility. Maxim Gorki, an early Communist writer, composed naturalistic dramas and tales describing the horrible living conditions of the poor working classes in cities.

During the early Soviet period Konstantin A. Fedin, Leonid M. Leontov, and Aleksandr Fadeyev aroused a great deal of interest with their novels. Later, a famous book entitled *And Quiet Flows the Don* by Mikhail A. Sholokhov was published. During the 1920s and 1930s, many prose writers were active in Soviet Russian literature. Mikhail Bulgakov wrote a series of sharp satires, followed by *The Master and Margarita*, which is regarded as one of the greatest novels written in this century. The humorous defiance in the novel was so strong that it was not published until the 1960s, more than twenty years after Bulgakov's death.

Mikhail Zoshchenko published short, biting stories that poked fun at everyday pretensions and pompous propaganda. For a long time his work was the most popular reading among average Soviet citizens. They loved his popular storytelling style.

Isaak Babel was a Jewish writer who evoked the colorful Jewish section of his native port city, Odessa, with all of its good-natured fun and mischief. He also described the early days of the Soviet army and its cossack riders in *Red Cavalry and Other Stories*.

One of Russia's most distinguished writers and poets of the twentieth century was Boris Pasternak. Copies of his 1957 novel, *Doctor Zhivago*, were hard to find in the Soviet state, but the book was widely circulated and read abroad. The book was made into a popular motion picture in the United States. In 1958 Pasternak won the Nobel Prize in literature, but refused to accept it, fearing that he might have to leave his beloved Russia forever.

Twentieth-century authors (left to right) are Maxim Gorki, Aleksandr Solzhenitsyn, and Boris Pasternak.

In 1962 Aleksandr Solzhenitsyn published *One Day in the Life of Ivan Denisovich*. It describes the experiences of inmates in a prison camp. His *Gulag Archipelago* is another such work. When Solzhenitsyn, too, received the Nobel Prize (in 1970), he was prohibited from accepting it until after the Soviet government exiled him in 1974.

In recent decades a few courageous, creative poets departed from the strict Communist themes. One of the best-known poets, Yevgeni Yevtushenko, wrote about becoming corrupt with the easy life and about the mistreatment of certain people. Andrei Voznesensky composed soul-searching verse about the harshness of city life. Nikolai Tikhonov showed his independence in realistic poems about romantic subjects.

The republics have famous writers also. Ivan Franko and Mikhail Kotsyubinsky are Ukrainian prose writers, and Ukrainian poets are Taras Shevchenko and Lesya Ukrainka. Kazakhstan authors include Mukhtar Auezov and Abdizhamil Murpeisov. Chizgiz Aitmatov from Kyrgyzstan and Tajikistan poet Mirzo Tursunzade are popular.

FILMMAKING

The film classic *Battleship Potemkin* made by Sergei Eisenstein in 1925 is considered by many to be one of the best films ever made. Filmmaking has always been important in Russia and still is. More than three hundred full-length films are produced each year. Every day eleven to twelve million people all over the country go to see films.

ART AND ARCHITECTURE

Russian art may be divided into four historical periods. The first era was Byzantine (from the tenth to the early sixteenth century), with its religious icons and decorative mosaics and frescoes. The Moscow, or National, Period, from the sixteenth to the eighteenth century, with emphasis on Russian saints and churches followed. Then came the European Period (1703-1917), with influences from painters and sculptors from various European countries, and finally the Soviet Period (1918-1989), when paintings were of the realistic school, reflecting socialist political thoughts and everyday events.

Dmitri Levitsky, Andrei Rublev, Orest Kiprensky, Karl Bryullov, Aleksandr Ivanov, Vasili Surikov, Kazimir Malevich, Arkady Plastov, Ilya Repin, Valentin Serov, and Mikhail Vrubel are regarded as Russia's most notable artists. Marc Chagall and Vasily Kandinsky also began their careers in Russia before emigrating abroad.

Gilded domes of the Church of the Deposition of the Robe in Moscow's Kremlin

Russian architecture corresponds with its art periods, as demonstrated by its forms and ornamental expressions on cathedrals, churches, palaces, theaters, and more recently designed buildings. Many of the fantastic structures in Moscow's Kremlin reflect each of the traditions prevalent when built. Here one will find buildings featuring arches supporting cupolas, onion-shaped domes, early Russian baroque characteristics, Byzantine designs, and Italian motifs. A number of buildings include classic columns, an expression of Russian nationalist art.

MUSIC

Soviet musical composers and artists have followed a great tradition of Russian excellence. The love of music is great in the Commonwealth. There are fifteen philharmonic societies and more than seven hundred symphony orchestras in the

Russians have excelled in music. Mstislav Rostropovich (left) is renowned as a cellist, conductor, and teacher. Peter Ilyich Tchaikovsky (center) and Sergei Prokofiev (right) are two well-known composers.

Commonwealth. Every year their concerts are attended by millions of people. Chamber music is also popular.

Two gifted composers, Dmitri Shostakovich and Sergei Prokofiev, have had tremendous influence on musical composition in today's world. Aram Khachaturian, an Armenian composer born in Georgia, is popular in the Commonwealth and abroad. Modest Mussorgsky, Peter Ilyich Tchaikovsky, and Nicholas Rimsky-Korsakov are other famous composers, along with Dmitri Kabalevsky and Tikhon Khrenikov. A number of Russian composers, including Sergei Rachmaninoff and Igor Stravinsky, left their country after the revolution and settled in the United States. Conductors and performers, among them Serge Koussevitsky, Vladimir Horowitz, Jascha Heifetz, Mstislav Rostropovich, and Nathan Milstein, left as well.

In February 1992, Boris Yeltsin, while on a visit to the United States, presented Mstislav Rostropovich with a medal. The anti-Communist cellist and conductor once again began to perform in his homeland.

The Moscow Circus is enjoyed by everyone.

OTHER FORMS OF RECREATION

Many different forms of recreation are offered in the Commonwealth. Animals draw crowds at aquariums and zoos, and just about every major city has a circus. There are many theaters in the various republics with a wide choice of productions ranging from tragedies to comedies. Moscow has a Theater for Young Spectators; elsewhere more than a hundred puppet theaters bring smiles and laughs to young audiences.

The Russian opera and ballet theaters have a history of excellence. The Bolshoi Ballet is more than two hundred years old. The company of one thousand has toured throughout the world. To become a leading dancer in the Bolshoi or Kirov troupe is the ultimate dream of countless girls and boys.

Chapter 10

LIVING IN THE COMMONWEALTH

The economy of Russia and the former republics of the Soviet Union has undergone profound changes. After communism failed, the Commonwealth republics tried to adopt more capitalist ways of doing business. They were slowed in reaching their objective by the reluctance of foreign governments and companies to invest in the Commonwealth. The steep rise in business and personal income taxes and the enormous debts of the large "enterprises," both to each other and to the banks, also helped retard economic progress. There was little knowledge or understanding on the part of factory and farm managers of how to run private operations. During the transition period a number of key industries still had to be controlled by the central government with Communist officials who were experts in their fields.

When Mikhail Gorbachev came to power he tried to move the economy away from that centralized system of control. He also tried to improve the quality of goods and set prices according to costs of production without government support. He encouraged businesses to make a profit. Workers were to be paid according to their ability and productivity. They would no longer be guaranteed jobs. Workers could be fired, which rarely occurred previously.

A paper mill in Bratsk, Russia

Massive state and collective farms were subdivided for more efficiency, private management, and worker profit sharing. Small farmers and craftsmen were allowed to sell their products for personal gain. Private ownership was accelerated. Individuals began to rely on the black market and barter to obtain merchandise difficult to find in the stores. People were allowed to perform private services for a fee and keep the income. Still, progress in the private sector lagged behind expectations well into the 1990s.

INDUSTRIAL SPECIALIZATION

Three-quarters of Russia's mineral and fuel wealth comes from the Urals, Siberia, and the Far East. This includes most of the oil, natural gas, coal, diamonds, and timber. Russia has practically every major mineral within its boundaries. There are large metal-refining plants, and manufacturing and processing facilities can be found within the republic.

An oil field in Armenia

Ukraine leads the republics with more than 150 industries. It is a major producer of iron ore, steel, nonferrous metals, and fuel. Vehicle manufacturing, machine-tool products, and home appliances make up a large segment of Belarus's economy. Moldova specializes in such industries as power engineering, farm equipment, electrical devices, and food processing.

In the Transcaucasian republics Azerbaijan has many oil and chemical refineries and is rich in minerals. Armenia produces much energy, has a very diversified manufacturing base, and is known for its marble and minerals extracted from the republic's mountains.

The Central Asian republics provide the Commonwealth with a wide variety of products. Kazakhstan provides power and fuel and has tremendous oil reserves. Kyrgyzstan is rich in minerals and has a number of silk and carpet-weaving factories. Textile manufacturing is important in Uzbekistan. Silk and carpet mills are found throughout Tajikistan.

MANUFACTURING

There is a concern about the quantity and quality of factorymade goods. The continued use of outdated machinery, old management ideas, and a centralized planning system slowed production. The republics are behind industrial nations in new technology with automation and use of computers.

Commonwealth economists hope that changes being introduced, especially profit sharing, will stimulate the growth of manufacturing. Industrial complexes are seeking partnerships, investors, and research and development assistance from abroad.

AGRICULTURE

Agriculture lags far behind industry. It is the weakest part of the economy, despite the fact that the Commonwealth ranks first in the world in a number of food crops. How to provide the large population with more than a basic amount of food remains a serious problem, as it has for centuries. The main farming regions are often hit by droughts. When the grain harvest is poor, livestock cannot be fed unless grain is purchased from other countries.

Private gardens are becoming important in the Commonwealth. Farmers spend time cultivating their own gardens. Though only about 2 to 3 percent of all agricultural land is worked privately, 30 percent of the production of vegetables, meat, milk, and eggs is thought to come from this source. Many farmers raise poultry on their private lots. Most of the produce is kept by the owners. The rest is sold on the free market for higher prices to buyers interested in better-quality food. The farmers keep the profits.

A tea plantation in the foothills of the Caucasus Mountains near the Black Sea

Although the territory of Russia and the Commonwealth is vast, less than one-fourth of it can be used for agricultural production. Most of the food is grown in European Russia. Wheat comes mostly from Ukraine, Kazakhstan, and southwestern Siberia. Cotton is a product of Central Asia. Tea, the national beverage, grows along the Black Sea coast, and sunflowers do well in Ukraine and the Ural regions.

The principal products grown in Russia are wheat, rye, barley, corn, oats, potatoes, cabbages, sugar beets, cotton, and flax. The Russian republic produces 53 percent of the Commonwealth's grain. Cattle, pigs, and sheep are raised on many Commonwealth farms.

In keeping with the reform movement, more farmlands are being transferred to individual and cooperative ownership with private management. Still, age-old problems persist. Some farmers still prefer the Communist-style communal approach where set salaries offset risk taking and hard work.

The former Soviet Union's amazing growth into one of the world's leading industrial powers is credited to its wealth of natural resources. The Commonwealth hopes this growth can be sustained. There are coal and gold mines, fields with bauxite and chromite, magnesium and manganese pits, and even silver and sulfur. Russia is rich in fuel, especially natural gas, as well as petroleum. Russian gas is exported to Europe.

Some regions of the Commonwealth have had their resources, especially coal and oil, depleted by years of excessive mining and pumping. Still, 70 percent of the CIS's hard coal and 58 percent of its steel come from the Russian republic. Russian geologists are encouraged by new discoveries of deposits of vital underground minerals throughout Siberia and the Far East. Russia is also the world's second largest diamond producer.

Three additional natural resources have proved important for the economy of Russia: the forest, furs, and fish. Russia leads all other republics in lumbering. Perhaps as much as 20 percent of the world's timber is located in the Commonwealth, and more than 80 percent of that is found in Siberia.

The fur industry has always been highly developed in Russia. Fur trapping and hunting extend over nearly one-half of the Commonwealth, but are mostly done in Siberia. Almost all of these activities are carried out during the winter months. Fur farms are becoming valuable sources for many kinds of pelts, some of which are exported after being processed. Mink, ermine, sable, and fox are highly valued and rare, but astrakhan, squirrel, and muskrat are sold in much greater quantities.

Russian fishermen are active all over the world, spending

A town on the Kamchatka Peninsula

months on end exploring the waters of the Indian, Atlantic, and Pacific oceans. Some trawlers have the capacity to serve as giant seagoing "fish factories." One, the *Riga*, has operated in recent years along the coast of Maine, buying fish from New England fishing fleets and processing it for Commonwealth markets. Tons of the fish caught are quickly cut up, processed, and canned or frozen aboard ship. The floating bases return to their home ports only when their hulls are full. Closer to home, in the cold Barents and White seas, cod, haddock, herring, and salmon are caught. Sturgeon is caught in the warmer waters of the Caspian Sea. The famous, expensive caviar is made from the eggs of sturgeon. Thousands of streams, rivers, and lakes are fishable every month of the year. Whales are still hunted for their oil in Pacific Ocean waters off the Kamchatka Peninsula.

The Yenisei River in Siberia

ENERGY PRODUCTION

A nation, no matter how wealthy in natural resources, cannot develop its industrial economy without energy and an efficient and reliable transportation system. The first Soviet planners realized that when drawing blueprints for industrial progress.

Russia is the only republic that appears to be self-sufficient in energy production. After the United States, Russia is the largest producer of electric energy in the world. Natural gas and water are plentiful and are used for generating electric power. Nuclear power stations have been constructed. On the Arctic Ocean, near Murmansk, the force of the tides is used to generate power. And in the warmer and sunnier parts of the Commonwealth there are experiments in solar energy use.

Russia and a number of Commonwealth republics are noted for their great potential for hydroelectric power. About 80 percent of it is concentrated in Central Asia, Siberia, and the Far East. The world's largest hydroelectric station is near Krasnoyarsk on the Yenisei River in Siberia.

Russia and the other Commonwealth states rely on nuclear

energy to produce much of their electricity. But two devastating nuclear accidents that took place at installations have caused considerable concern about the safety of nuclear plants. One took place near Chelyabinsk in the 1950s in the southern Ural Mountains. The second was the infamous explosion at Chernobyl, near Kiev in Ukraine, in April 1986. Both accidents left the surrounding areas nuclear wastelands. A disastrous earthquake in Armenia in December 1988 brought a halt to the completion of several nuclear reactors in that republic.

COMMUNICATION

Before glasnost the mass media was tightly controlled by Communist officials. Propaganda favorable to the USSR was used extensively to report and manage the news and to communicate a single point of view. The Soviet Union boasted of publishing 8,400 newspapers and 5,200 magazines. The literacy rate was 99 percent—one of the highest in the world. Radio and television broadcasting was state owned, and programs were designed to promote government interests. Today, restrictions have been dropped and the government no longer tries to manage the news.

In 1985, 23 percent of Soviet urban families and 7 percent of rural families had telephones. This number has increased. There are more than ninety million television sets in the Commonwealth and more than 150 million people watch the nightly news. Interest has risen in Western films and television programs.

TRANSPORTATION

The transport system in the Commonwealth is quite efficient, considering the need to ship goods and move passengers over

A section of the Trans-Siberian Railroad

great distances and challenging terrain during extreme weather conditions.

Railways handle the bulk of the freight. Russia and the Commonwealth have one-tenth of the world's railway tracks, but account for more than half of the world's total rail freight traffic.

The Baikal-Amur Mainline (BAM) was completed in October 1984. It is of tremendous importance to Siberia and all of Russia. It connects Lake Baikal with the Amur River in the Russian Far East, a distance of 2,000 miles (3,219 kilometers). The railroad runs from 100 to 200 miles (161 to 322 kilometers) north of the overburdened Trans-Siberian Railroad. Started in 1974, it was an incredible task. Most of the route is in the permafrost zone. Parts of mountains had to be blown away. Ice valleys had to be crossed. Tunnels, some up to 9 miles (14 kilometers) long, had to be dug. Miles of bridges had to be constructed. Snow and ice blocks 1,000 feet (305 meters) deep had to be melted by jet flames. There were

Aeroflot airplanes at the Moscow International Airport

other hardships and battles for the tens of thousands of workers. In addition to the cold winter and the devastating attacks by swarms of mosquitoes in the summer, the work brigades had to contend with more than 1,500 earthquakes. BAM carries vital fuels, minerals, and timber across the Siberian taiga to the industrial centers.

Trucks carry mostly short-haul farm products or manufactured cargo, but only about 8 percent of all freight is transported over Commonwealth roads on trucks. Trucks, particularly in Siberia, actually use frozen rivers as highways during the cold winter months.

Since the 1960s most of the Commonwealth's oil and gas have been transported by a growing network of pipelines from major deposits in Siberia to western Russia and eastward to the Pacific coast.

The national airline of Russia and the republics, Aeroflot, accounts for 20 percent of all airline passengers flown on domestic and international flights in the world. Aeroflot carries millions of tons of cargo, too. Throughout the country planes are able to fly

Railway and bus terminal in Sochi

over harsh climatic conditions that bring other forms of
transportation to a standstill.

Past modes of surface transportation—sleds, wagons, and
carriages pulled by dogs, mules, horses, and reindeer—have
largely given way to motorized vehicles. The bus has become the
intercity transporter of people in the Commonwealth. Buses carry
more than three times as many passengers as do the railways and
one hundred times as many as the airlines.

The merchant marine is growing rapidly. Traditionally, Russia
was a landlocked country with few opportunities to trade with
countries overseas. Now vessels sail the seven seas. In the last few
years Russia has become a leading maritime power, despite the
fact that there are few ports, most of which are not free of ice in
the winter.

The long Arctic coast is icebound about nine months of the
year, but in 1977 the world's most powerful atomic icebreaker, the
Artika, broke a path to the North Pole. It took the Soviet ship
thirteen days and nights to get to the top of the world and return
to Murmansk, its home base. It sailed through solid ice.

The possibility of opening frozen sealanes in the Arctic is

important to the Commonwealth as it races to develop new frontier regions in the Arctic and Siberia.

All major rivers in Russia flow through flat country, but they too are frozen from four to ten months of the year, depending on their location. That is why river transport accounts for a relatively small part of the country's freight traffic. In an attempt to move more materials and goods more rapidly and consistently, more boats and barges have been added to the interior "river highway" fleets. River vessels carry tremendous amounts of freight over 78,295 miles (126,000 kilometers) of inland waters.

Transporting people and goods in an area the size of the Commonwealth is difficult. But much has been accomplished in mastering distance and overcoming natural barriers. In recent times Soviet engineers, scientists, and transportation specialists have made remarkable progress on land, sea, and air. Beneath the ground marvelous subways have been built.

FOREIGN TRADE

Despite the fact that the Commonwealth is a world power, its exports are mainly based on raw materials, especially oil, gas, and coal. This is a serious problem, for the Commonwealth nations desperately need hard currency, like dollars and other Western money, required to purchase scarce consumer products and hi-tech equipment for their factories.

ENVIRONMENTAL PROBLEMS

The Commonwealth has serious problems with air and water pollution. Soft coal is used to generate much electric power. Older

The Commonwealth has serious problems with air pollution.

smokestack refineries and factories pollute the air, as do the
emissions from automobiles and trucks, which are not equipped
with pollution controls. People living near industrial plants have
suffered serious health problems over the years. Only limited
measures, like the planting of vegetation, have been taken to
improve the air quality.

Years of dumping sewage and waste into the rivers, lakes, and
streams of the Commonwealth have taken their toll on the
environment. Pesticides found their way into water supplies,
contaminating or killing fish. Russia claims it must continue to
dump A-waste into oceans until 1996, when its system for disposal
should be developed.

SPACE EXPLORATION

The people of the former Soviet Union earned their greatest
pride with the accomplishments of their space program, and many

A photograph of Yuri Gagarin and the space capsule he used to orbit the earth in 1961

in the Commonwealth hope these achievements will continue. The Soviet Union was the first nation to launch a satellite. In 1957 *Sputnik* was put in orbit. After experimenting with sending animals and plants into space, Yuri Gagarin, in 1961, became the first cosmonaut to orbit the earth. A year later Valentina Tereshkova became the first female cosmonaut in space.

In 1984 new crews of cosmonauts were launched from the Soviet space center at Baikonur in Kazakhstan in Central Asia. In that year three separate manned spacecraft were sent up to dock with the orbiting space station *Salyut 7*. Their crews conducted scientific experiments in outer space.

In June 1985 planetary weather balloons with instrument packages began sending data on the clouds and winds of Venus after being dropped into the planet's atmosphere. The balloons had been dropped by Soviet spacecraft en route to a meeting with Halley's Comet in March 1986.

This impressive monument to space exploration is in Moscow.

The exploration balloon, a first of its kind, floated at an altitude of about 33 miles (53 kilometers) above the surface of Venus. It transmitted signals revealing scientific data about atmospheric conditions there. The signals were "read" by cooperating radio telescopes around the world.

Soviet cosmonauts set amazing records for time in space. Two men stayed in space for nearly 366 days in 1987-1988. It is interesting to note that when Sergei Krikalev blasted off into outer space on May 18, 1991, the Soviet Union was still intact. When he landed in Kazakhstan 311 days later, the USSR no longer existed.

In 1992 Russian space officials, envisioning Russians and Americans setting foot on Mars together, offered the United States use of their *Mir* space station. In the spirit of cooperation in space, they also offered their *Soyuz* spacecraft as an emergency crew rescue vehicle for the proposed American space station. The Russians also proposed joint satellite efforts to monitor weapons

A fresh stream in the Caucasus Mountains

and missile technologies of other countries. In addition, a space platform equipped with mirrors to divert radiation from the earth and more sunlight to it was proposed and positioned in space. Although experimental, it was thought that the platform could also be used to clean up space debris or reconstruct the ozone layer. Russia and Commonwealth countries are pursuing a policy of cooperation and collaboration in space programs.

THE FUTURE OF THE COMMONWEALTH

The dramatic changes that took place in the Soviet Union in the mid-1980s and the founding of the Commonwealth of

Faces of the Commonwealth of Independent States

Independent States could be the start of a successful union of
former Soviet republics, but there are many tensions between
them and the forging of a successful, permanent commonwealth
will take much hard work.

For centuries past, the people of this region have suffered
oppression, civil strife, and the perils of war. Learning the lessons
of history, many now prefer to resolve differences peacefully,
through dialogue, compromise, and mutual understanding. Their
wish is that an ancient Russian proverb will finally be adhered to:
"Wag your tongue as much as you please, but don't wave your
gun."

MAP KEY (Does not include the states of Belarus, Ukraine, and Moldova)

Aldan, *river*	C7, D7
Alma-Ata	F4
Amur, *river*	E7, E8
Anadyrskiy Zaliv, *bay*	A8
Angara, *river*	D5
Aral Sea	E2, E3
Arctic Circle	A7, B7
Arctic Ocean	A4, A5
Arkhangel'sk (Archangel)	C3
Armenia, *state*	E1
Ashkhabad	F2
Astrakhan	E2
Azerbaijan, *state*	E1
Azovskoye More (Sea of Azov)	D1
Baikal, Lake (Ozero Baykal)	D6, E6
Baku	E1
Barents Sea	B3
Bering Sea	A8, B8
Bering Strait	A7, A8
Bishkek	F3
Black Sea	D1, E1
Blagoveshchensk	D7
Braskoye Vdkhr, *lake*	D5
Bukhara	F3
Caspian Depression	E2
Caspian Sea	E2, F1, F2
Caucasus Mountains	E1
Chita	E6
Chukotskiy P-OV, *peninsula*	A7, A8
Don, *river*	D1, D2
Dushanbe	F3
Dzhugdzhur Kherbet, *mountains*	C7, D7
East Siberian Sea	A6, A7, B6, B7
Gur'yev	E2
Indigirka, *river*	B7, C7
Irkutsk	E6
Irtysh, *river*	E4
Ishim, *river*	D3, E3
Kapchagay	F4
Kara Sea	B4, C4
Kazakhstan, *state*	D2, D3, E2, E3, E4, F3
Kazan	D2
Khabarovsk	D8
Khrebet Gydan, *mountains*	B7, C7
Kirghiz Steppe	E2, E3
Kokand	F3
Kolskiy P-OV, *peninsula*	B3, C3
Kolyma, *river*	B7
Komandorskiye Ostrova	B8
Komsomolsk	D8
Koryakskiy Kherbet, *mountains*	B8
Krasnoyarsk	D5
Kuril Islands	C8, D8
Kyrgyzstan, *state*	F3, F4
Kyzyl	E5
Ladozhskove Ozero, *lake*	C2
Laptev Sea	B5, B6
Lena, *river*	B6, C6, C7
Mary	F2
M. Chelyuskin, *island*	B5
M. Dezhneva (East Cape)	A7, A8
M. Lopatka, *island*	C8
Moscow	C2
Nerchinsk	E6
Nizhny Novgorod	D2
Nizhnyaya Tunguska, *river*	C5, D5
North Pole	A4, B4
Novaya Zemlya, *island*	B3, B4, C3, C4
Novosibirsk	E4
Novosibirskiye O-Va (New Siberian Islands)	B6
Ob, *river*	C3, D3, D4
Obskava Guba, *sea*	C4
Okhotsk	C7
Okhotsk, Sea of	C7, C8
Olenek, *river*	B6, C5, C6
Omsk	D4
Onezhvkove Ozero, *lake*	C2
Orenburg	D2
Ozero Balkhask, *lake*	E3, E4
Pamirs, *mountains*	F3
Perm	D3
Pervyy Kuril'skiy Prol.	C8
Petropavlovsk-Kamchatskiy	C8
Plato Ust-Urt	E2
P-OV Kamchatka, *peninsula*	C8
P-OV Taymyr, *peninsula*	B5
Rostov-na-donu (Rostov-on-Don)	D1
Russia, *state*	A7, A8, B2, B3, B4, B5, B6, B7, B8, C1, C2, C3, C4, C5, C6, C7, C8, D1, D2, D3, D4, D5, D6, D7, D8, E1, E2, E4, E5, E6, E8
Sakhalin, *island*	D8
Samara	D2
Samarkand	F3
Sayan Khrebet, *mountains*	E5
Semipalatinak	E4
Sev Dvina, *river*	C3
Severnaya Zemlya (Northern Land), *island*	B5
Siberia	A7, A8, B4, B5, B6, B7, B8, C4, C5, C6, C7, C8, D4, D5, D6, D7, D8, E4, E5, E6
Sikhote Alin	D8, E8
Soya Kaikyo	D8
Sovetskaya Gavan	D8
Stanovoy Khrebet, *mountains*	D7
St. Petersburg (Leningrad)	C2
Syr Dar'ya, *river*	E3, F3
Tajikistan, *state*	F3
Tashkent	F3
Tatar Strait	D8
Tayshet	D5
Tbilisi	E1
Tien Shan, *mountains*	F4
Tobol'sk	D3
Tomsk	D4
Tselinograd	E3
Turkestan	E2, F2, F3
Tungusky, *river*	C5, D6
Turkmenistan, *state*	E2, F2, F3
Ural, *river*	D2, E2
Urals, *mountains*	C3, D3
Uzbekistan, *state*	E2, F2, F3
Verkhoyansk	C6
Verkhoyanskiy Khrebet, *mountains*	C6, C7
Vladivostok,	E8
Volga, *river*	D2, D3
Vrangelya (Wrangel), *island*	A7
Yablonovyy Kherbet, *mountains*	D6, E6
Yakutsk	C7
Yana, *river*	B6, C6
Yenisey, (Yenisei) *river*	C4, C5
Yeniseysk	D5
Yekaterinburg	D3
Yerevan	E1
Zemlya Frantsa-Iosifa (Franz Josef Land), *island*	B4

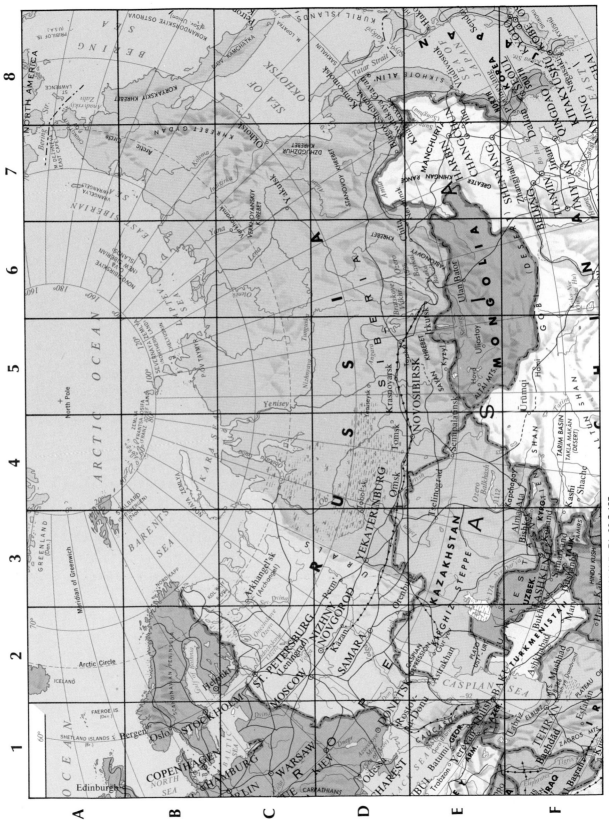

Map from Quick Reference World Atlas, © 1993 by Rand McNally, R.L. 92-S-197

MINI-FACTS AT A GLANCE

GENERAL INFORMATION

Official Name: Commonwealth of Independent States (CIS) (*Sodruzhestvo Nezavisimykh Gosudarstv*)

Administrative Center: Minsk

Government: The CIS is not a state but a community of independent states organized by the successor states of the former Union of Soviet Socialist Republics (USSR). In December 1991 the Soviet Union with its Communist system of government ceased to exist, and 11 of the former 15 Soviet republics formed a new federation of independent states, united by common interests. Each of the 11 states has its own constitution and government. Member states of the CIS are Armenia, Azerbaijan, Belarus, Kazakhstan, Kyrgyzstan, Moldova, Russia, Tajikistan, Turkmenistan, Ukraine, and Uzbekistan. Estonia, Latvia, and Lithuania did not take part in the founding negotiations of the CIS, and Georgia was represented only by observers.

Constitution: According to the founding members of the CIS, its common affairs are to be regulated on a multilateral, interstate basis rather than by central institutions. CIS will have no common citizenship, no president, and no parliament elected by the commonwealth as a whole; it will provide only a framework for military and foreign policy and economic coordination. According to the Alma-Ata Declaration on December 21, 1991, the "supreme organ" of CIS is a Council of Heads of States. This organ is associated with a Council of Heads of Governments.

Religion: The CIS has no official religion. In 1991 about 37 percent of the population of its members followed Christianity, out of which Orthodox Christians were 32 percent, Protestants 3 percent, and Roman Catholics 2 percent. Some 13 percent of the population follows Islam. Less than 1 percent of the population is Jewish, and less than 0.5 percent follows Buddhism and other religions. Some 30 percent is nonreligious, and about 19 percent is atheist.

Ethnic Composition: There are more than 100 nationalities with their own history, languages, traditions, and customs. Russians are the largest ethnic group accounting for almost 52 percent of the population, followed by Ukrainians, 16 percent; Uzbeks, 6 percent; Belorussians, 3.5 percent; Kazakhs, 3 percent; Azerbaijanis, 2.5 percent; Tatars, 2.5 percent; Armenians, 1.7 percent; Tajiks, 1.5 percent; and others, 11.3 percent. The Kazakhs are Muslims of Mongol descent who speak a Turkic language. Azerbaijanis are famous for their elderly population; the average age of the population is 76 years.

Language: Russian is spoken and read in most of the CIS, but is no longer regarded as a "common" language. Each state has its own official language. Byelorussian, Ukrainian, Armenian, Finnish, Turkic, Kurdish, and Yiddish are also used outside the borders of individual CIS republics. Like many Slavic languages, Russian, Byelorussian, and Ukrainian are written in Cyrillic script. In all 130 different languages are spoken throughout the states of the CIS.

National Flag, Emblem, and Anthem: There is no one official flag, emblem, or anthem of the CIS. Each member state has its own state flag, emblem, and anthem.

National Calendar: The Gregorian Calendar has been in use since 1918.

Money: The Russian ruble (100 *kopecks*) is the currency of Russia and is used by other member states of the CIS as well, although it is not legal tender in many places, including Ukraine. Member states have introduced, or announced the introduction of, their own currencies. In late 1991 1 ruble was equal to $1.69 in United States currency. In March 1994, about 1,677 rubles were equal to $1 U.S.

Membership in International Organization: Individual republics of the CIS have membership in the United Nations and some in the World Bank. Russia is a member of UN Security Council.

Weights and Measures: The CIS uses the metric system.

Population: 288,600,000 (1991); Density is 32.9 persons per sq. mi. (12.7 persons per sq km); 66 percent urban, 34 percent rural.

Cities:

Moscow	8,801,500
St. Petersburg (Leningrad)	4,466,800
Kiev	2,635,000
Tashkent	2,113,300
Baku	1,713,300
Minsk	1,633,600
Kharkov	1,622,800
Novosibirsk	1,446,300
Nizhny Novgorod (Gorky)	1,445,000
Ekaterinburg (Sverdlovsk)	1,375,400
Tbilisi	1,279,000

```
Samara (Kuybyshev)................................ 1,257,300
Yerevan ........................ 1,199,000  (1989 estimate)
Dnepropetrovsk ................................... 1,189,300
Almaty ........................................... 1,156,200
Chelyabinsk ...................................... 1,148,300
Rostov-on-Don .................................... 1,127,600
Donetsk .......................................... 1,121,300
Kazan ............................................ 1,107,300
Perm ............................................. 1,100,400
Ufa............................................... 1,097,000
Volgograd ........................................ 1,007,300
Saratov ..........................................   911,100
Voronezh .........................................   900,000
```
(Population based on 1991 estimates.)

GEOGRAPHY

Mountains: Major mountain ranges include the Pamirs, the Carpathians, the mountains of the Caucasus and the Crimea, and the Urals. The Tien Shan Mountains are snowcapped throughout the year. The Pamir range in the southeast has some of the highest mountain peaks in the CIS.

Highest Point: Communism Peak, 24,590 ft. (7,495 m) (not yet renamed)

Lowest Point: Karagiye Depression, 433 ft. (132 m) below sea level

Rivers: The Volga is the longest (2,194 mi; 3,531 km) river in Europe. Other rivers are the Dniester, Dnieper, Don, Ob, Yenisei, Lena, and Irtysh. Siberian rivers freeze to depths of 9 ft. (2.7 m) and are used in wintertime as highways by heavy trucks. Most of the Central Asian rivers dry up before reaching any body of water. A network of canals provides opportunities for farming in this semidesert; Kara-Kum Canal in Turkmenistan is one of the world's foremost water development projects.

Lake: Lake Baikal in southeastern Siberia contains 20 percent of all the freshwater resources on earth. It is the deepest (5,315 ft.; 1,620 m) continental lake in the world. The Caspian Sea is the world's largest inland body of water and a salt lake. Some of the reclaimed Pripyat Marshes in Belarus are used for agriculture.

Forests: Almost 45 percent of the land is under forests, with an additional 15 percent under meadows and pastures. As much as 20 percent of the world's timber is located in the CIS. *Taiga*, an east-west band of thick evergreen forests, extends for 5,000 mi. (8,047 km) in northern Siberia. Chief deciduous and evergreen trees are spruce, pine, fir, ash, oak, poplar, chestnut, birch, beech, larch, hornbeam, cedar, maple, and linden. In the arid southern region short grasses, scrub, palm, bamboo, and cactus prevail. Russia leads other states in lumbering.

Wildlife: CIS has a wide variety of animals, including white bear, sea hares, walruses, polar foxes, reindeer, lemmings, elks, brown bear, lynx, sable, boars, deer, wildcats, marmots, polecats, mountain goats, porcupines, leopards, hyenas, and wolves. Fur trapping and hunting extend over nearly one-half of the CIS, but is mostly concentrated in Siberia where a great variety of fur-bearing animals are found. Many kinds of animals, like mink, ermine, fox, astrakhan, squirrel, and muskrat, are raised on fur farms.

Birds: Bird life includes sea gulls, loons, white partridges, polar owls, geese, swans, ducks, crossbills, nutcrackers, cuckoos, woodpeckers, kestrels, cranes, eagles, larks, turkey hens, partridges, pheasants, and desert ravens.

Climate: The CIS extends over an enormous area. It has several different climate zones—from Arctic tundra in the north to desert lowland in the south. Rainfall is highest in areas bordering the Baltic and Black seas, Caspian Sea, and the eastern coast of Asiatic Russia. In the southern dry region, rainfall is usually less than 8 in. (20 cm) annually; summer temperatures in this part can be well over 100° F (37.7° C) for weeks. The semiarid steppe region has hot and dry summers. The climate of Russia is continental with a wide variation in summer and winter temperatures. Winters are generally very cold throughout the CIS. Verkhoyansk in northern Siberia is the coldest spot on earth—with average January temperatures of minus 60° F. (minus 51.2° C). In western Siberia snow stays on the ground for 140 to 260 days or more. The Arctic has little daylight in winter. In the European Plain region summers are warm and winters are cold.

Greatest Distance: North to South: 3,200 mi. (5,150 km)
East to West: 6,000 mi. (9,656 km)

ECONOMY AND INDUSTRY

Agriculture: Collectively, the member states of the CIS rank first in the world in a number of food crops. Areas under agriculture and permanent cultivation amount roughly to 11 percent. Massive state and collective farms are being subdivided for more efficiency, private management, and worker profit sharing. Private ownership of land is being accelerated; private gardens are popular.
The steppe is one of the world's outstanding wheat-growing areas. Chief agricultural products of the CIS are wheat, sugar beets, potatoes, barley, rye, oats, corn, cabbage, peas, cotton, sunflower seeds, millet, rice, fruits (grapes, apricots, plums, pears, oranges, peaches), flax, tobacco, and both green and black tea leaves.

Moldova contains nearly one-fourth of the CIS's vineyards. Irrigation is essential in the dry Asian region where drought presents a serious threat periodically. Rice, grapes, and other fruits are grown—with irrigation—in Uzbekistan.

Livestock: Cattle, pigs, and sheep are raised on most farms. In Kyrgyzstan, the breeding of fine-fleeced sheep, pedigreed horses, and yaks is important. Horses are still used for some transportation in Turkmenistan. Astrakhan furs (lamb's fur) are produced in Uzbekistan.

Fishing: Cod, haddock, herring, salmon, smelt, sturgeon, and whales are caught in the Barents, White, and Caspian seas, and the Pacific Ocean. The famous expensive caviar is made from the eggs of sturgeon. The chief freshwater fish are carp, bream, pike, perch, and vendace.

Mining: The states of the CIS have almost every major mineral within their boundaries. Minerals come largely from the Urals, Siberia, and the Far East (Russia). Chief minerals are coal, petroleum, asbestos, zinc, copper, lead, bauxite, chromite, magnesium, nickel, molybdenum, tungsten, silver, gold, mercury, sulfur, and diamonds. Some 60 percent of CIS's coal reserves, iron mines, and oil is found in Ukraine. The Tengiz oil field in Kazakhstan is one of the largest in the world. Russia is one of the largest producer of hydroelectric energy in the world. The world's largest hydroelectric plant is near Krasnoyarsk on the Yenisei River in Siberia.

Manufacturing: The chief manufactured items are steel, cement, pig iron, fertilizer, sulfuric acid, food products, sugar, cellulose, paper and paperboard, plastics, soda ash, man-made fibers, machine tools, medical equipment, food-processing equipment, vehicles, farm equipment, tires, television and radio receivers, washing machines, refrigerators, bicycles, cars, and tractors.

Handicrafts: Every nationality in the CIS has a long tradition of handicrafts. Turkmenistan produces fine handmade carpets. Small handpainted lacquered boxes; *matrioshka*, Russian nesting dolls; bone carvings; woolen kerchiefs; porcelain figures; and hand-embroidered clothing are the most popular handicrafts. Gem-studded belts and gold-threaded shawls are made in Azerbaijan. The *kamuz*, a three-stringed musical instrument, is crafted in Kirghiz.

Transportation: Railways and pipelines are very important for the CIS as road building is complicated by the harsh climate. Railways handle the bulk of the freight. Before the breakup of the former USSR there were about 92,000 mi. (148,056 km) of railroad tracks, and about 612,000 mi. (984,892 km) of roads. Almost 90 percent of the roads are paved. The Baikal-Amur Mainline (BAM) railway in Russia carries vital fuels, minerals, and timber across the Siberian taiga to industrial centers. Most of the large cities have subways. Kiev has a funicular, a cable railway system. St. Petersburg is the largest seaport on the Baltic Sea.

Vladivostok is one of the largest naval bases and seaports on the Pacific Ocean. Aeroflot is the major domestic and international airline. Since the formation of CIS, many of Aeroflot's subsidiaries have established themselves as independent airlines; there were as many as 69 airlines in CIS in 1992.

Communication: Almost every household has a television set, and about 30 percent have telephones. Radio and television broadcasting is no longer state owned, and the government no longer tries to manage the news. *Izvestia*, the Communist government newspaper, became independent in 1992. *Pravda*, the newspaper of the party, was forced by economic circumstances to drastically limit its circulation in early 1992. The *New York Times* began publishing the Russian language *New York Times in Review* in several cities in April 1992. Filmmaking was very important in the former Soviet Union; every day, some 11 to 12 million people go to see films.

Trade: Republics of the CIS export mostly raw materials such as oil, gas, and coal. The major export items are crude petroleum and petroleum products, natural gas, heavy machinery, fertilizers, chemicals, wood, and paper products. Chief export destinations are Germany, Romania, Italy, Japan, Poland, Finland, France, Hungary, China, and India. The chief import items are machinery and transport equipment, consumer goods, cereals and food products, chemicals, textiles, and clothing. Major import sources are Germany, the United States, Romania, India, Finland, Poland, Japan, and Hungary.

EVERYDAY LIFE

Health: Most health care is free, but it is subject to each member state's guidelines. Diseases of the circulatory and respiratory system and cancer are among the major causes of death. In addition to hospitals and clinics, holiday homes and sanitoria (mostly for patients with tuberculosis) are available. Special clinics take care of children up to the age of sixteen.

Education: Education in the states of the CIS is compulsory, fairly uniform, and highly structured. Textbooks may be written in as many as fifty-two different languages. Formal education begins at age six and continues until age seventeen. Children attend classes six days a week and discipline is strict. Teachers are respected and honored; weekly progress reports are sent home. Children with outstanding skills, abilities, and talents attend many kinds of specialized schools. All students must take a national examination at the end of the eighth grade. Higher scoring students eventually pursue professional studies and lower scoring students go on to vocational high schools. In Siberia correspondence courses are quite common due to the great distances between homes and schools. The literacy rate in the early 1990s was almost 99 percent—one of the highest in the world.

Akademgorodok is an academic town in Siberia with a national research center. Almost all of its population is engaged in education-related activities.

Holidays:
January 1, New Year's Day
March 8, International Women's Day
May 1-2, May Day
May 9, Victory Day
June 25, Festival of the Plow
September 1, Teacher's Day
September 12, Mushroom Harvest Day
November 7-8, October Revolution
December 25, Christmas
December, Poetry Day

Some holidays vary from state to state.

Culture: The states of the CIS have rich literary traditions. Moscow is the political and cultural center of the CIS. The Kremlin, Bolshoi Theater, St. Basil's Church, Lenin's Mausoleum, Moscow University, the GUM department store, and the underground Metro rail are chief attractions. The Hermitage Winter Palace in St. Petersburg is one of the world's greatest fine arts museums. Samarkand and Bukhara are richly endowed with mosques with colorful tiled turquoise and gold towers. CIS has some fifteen philharmonic societies and over seven hundred symphony orchestras. Poetry recitals are very popular throughout the CIS.

Housing: There is a serious housing shortage in the CIS, and construction of new housing complexes has been slow in recent years. A single-family home in cities is often used by more than one family. The majority of urban dwellers live in high-rise apartment complexes. Almost every urban household has access to electricity, public water supply, and central heating.

People in rural areas live in small farmhouses, log houses, wood cottages, stone buildings, or *yurts*, circular tents made of felt or skins on a framework of poles (mostly used by nomadic herders). The furnishings are usually simple but functional, with decorative rugs on the walls. The windows of the village houses are often decorative, and are generally enclosed by hand-carved frames. A fenced-in backyard garden provides vegetables, grapes, and sunflowers, and also serves as barn to the family cow, chickens, geese, and ducks.

Family and Society: Both parents in a family usually work. Except for mining, women hold the same jobs as men. Seventy-five percent of the doctors are women. Grandmothers, endearingly called *babushkas*, are credited with holding society together. In Central Asian states marriages are generally arranged by parents.

Divorce is readily obtained by Muslim men but almost never by a woman. Large families are common in Tajikistan, a predominantly Muslim state. Muslim women do not work outside the home.

Society in the CIS is largely made up of industrial-management personnel, professionals, and farm workers. With the end of the Communist system, opportunities for upward social and geographic mobility are breaking traditional social barriers. Life-styles, especially for younger people, have changed.

Food: Food varies with nationality and availability. In most places, lunch is the largest meal of the day. In general the diet is low on meat and dairy products. Bread, sausages, canned fish, cabbage, potatoes, and beets are the most common food items. In the Slavic states cabbage and potatoes are staple foods. *Borscht,* a soup made with beets; *rassolinik,* fish soup; sour cream; and *kasha,* a cereal grain, are favorites in the Russian diet. *Pirozhkis* are fried or baked rolls filled with meat or cabbage. A mutton and rice mixture, *plov,* is popular in Central Asia. Moldovan diets include lamb dishes, cheese, barley porridge, and chestnut meal or corn meal. Sweet Ukrainian dumplings are filled with fruit and are served with sour cream. Lamb kebabs, chicken, fish, rice pilaf, goat cheese, olives, grapes, and vegetable-filled pita-type bread are popular in the Transcaucasian states. The food in southern states is similar to that found in Turkey or Greece. Horse and reindeer meat is eaten in Siberia. A *samovar,* or family teapot, supplies the beverage for the meal. Tea is the most common beverage. Vodka and wine are used in some homes. *Kvas* is a summer drink made by fermenting rye or barley.

Sports and Recreation: A variety of sports are popular in the CIS. Soccer, basketball, swimming, volleyball, ice hockey, tennis, wrestling, gymnastics, and track and field are some of the common conventional games. Reindeer and dog team races are popular in the cold northern latitudes. Horseback games, mountain climbing, boxing, and field hockey are popular in Kazakhstan, judo in Azerbaijan, and archery and fencing are popular in Tajikistan.

Major leisure activities are attending movies, seminars and lectures, concerts, and the theater; playing basketball, ice hockey, or soccer; taking ballet lessons; visiting museums, zoos, circuses, and parks; hiking; and camping. Chess is the favorite pastime for Russians of all ages. Pyatigorsk and Sochi are well-known health and recreation resorts in the Caucasus.

IMPORTANT DATES

782 B.C.—The city of Yerevan is founded

A.D. 350—Armenia becomes the first state to adopt Christianity

1067—The city of Minsk is founded

1581–Yermak leads expedition to Siberia, defeats the Tatars

1589–The city of Volgograd is founded as Tsaritsyn

1613–Beginning of Romanov dynasty

1628–Krasnoyarsk is founded as a fort city

1703–Tsar Peter the Great establishes the city of St. Petersburg

1812–Napoleon Bonaparte invades Russia

1854–The city of Alma-Ata is founded

1865-1885–Russia establishes control over Central Asia

1867–Russia sells Alaska to the United States

1891-1905–The Trans-Siberian Railroad is built

1894–Nicholas II becomes Russia's last tsar

1907–Russia, England, and France form Triple Entente

1911-1913–Series of Balkan Wars

1914–Outbreak of World War I

1917–Revolutions in February and October; Tsar Nicholas II abdicates

1918–Treaty of Brest-Litovsk ends World War I on the eastern front; the tsar
and his family are executed; Russian Civil War begins; a constitution is announced

1919–The *Comintern* (Communist International) is established

1921–Russian Civil War ends

1922–First All-Union Congress is held; a federation of four republics establishes
the Union of Soviet Socialist Republics (USSR)

1924–Four more republics join the federation (USSR); Lenin dies

1929–Tadzhik republic joins the federation (USSR); first five-year plan begins

1932-33–Famine in USSR

1933–Adolf Hitler takes control in Germany

1934–USSR joins the League of Nations

1936–Kazakh and Kirghiz people are given republics

1939–Hitler invades Poland, World War II begins; USSR invades Poland and Finland

1940–Estonia, Latvia, and Lithuania are annexed as republics; Finland surrenders, giving up some territory

1941–Germany invades USSR, beginning of 900-day siege of Leningrad (St. Petersburg)

1942-43–The Battle of Stalingrad

1944–The siege of Leningrad ends

1945–World War II ends; Ukraine becomes a charter member of the United Nations

1948–West Berlin is blockaded by the Soviets

1949–USSR establishes COMECON (Council for Mutual Economic Assistance); formation of NATO (North Atlantic Treaty Organization)

1953–Joseph Stalin dies; Nikita Khrushchev becomes head of the Communist party

1954–The Crimea is added to the Ukraine Republic

1956–Revolts in Hungary and Poland

1957–*Sputnik I*, world's first spacecraft, is put in orbit

1961–Kremlin Palace of Congresses is erected; Berlin Wall is erected (demolished 1990); Yuri Gagarin becomes first man in space

1962–Cuban missile crisis; Valentina Tereshkova becomes the first female cosmonaut in space

1963–The US, USSR, and Great Britain sign treaty banning nuclear weapons tests except those underground

1964–Tashkent is destroyed by an earthquake; world's tenth-largest hydroelectric plant is built near Bratsk

1968–Soviet troops invade Czechoslovakia

1972–The USSR and US sign treaty to limit production of nuclear weapons

1974–Soviet government exiles author Aleksandr Solzhenitsyn; work begins on Baikal-Amur Mainline (BAM), north of the Trans-Siberian Railroad

1977–The world's most powerful atomic icebreaker, *Artika*, breaks a path to the North Pole

1979–USSR and US sign an arms limitation treaty (SALT II); USSR becomes involved in war in Afghanistan

1980–Olympic games are held in Moscow; the games are boycotted by the US

1984–USSR declines to participate in the Olympic games held in Los Angeles, California; the Baikal-Amur Mainline (BAM) is ready for operation.

1985–Mikhail Gorbachev becomes the official leader of the Soviet Union; Boris Yeltsin is chosen Communist leader of Moscow

1986–A disastrous nuclear accident occurs at Chernobyl, Ukraine

1987-88–Two Soviet cosmonauts spend 366 days in space

1988–Economic crisis grips the Soviet Union; violent ethnic fighting and territorial dispute begins in Nagorno-Karabakh region of Azerbaijan

1989–Moldova changes back to Roman characters from the Cyrillic alphabet

1990–Central Committee issues policies guaranteeing human rights

1991–Union of Soviet Socialist Republics is officially terminated; the Alma-Ata Declaration is signed by eleven former Soviet republics; the Commonwealth of Independent States is organized by the former eleven republics; Estonia, Latvia, and Lithuania proclaim a full separation from the Soviet Union; Leningrad is renamed St. Petersburg and Frunze is renamed Bishkek

1992–Ten states from the CIS are admitted to the International Monetary Fund and the World Bank; prices are deregulated and costs of goods and services are freed; Yeltsin visits the United States; Winter Olympics at Albertville, France, and Summer Olympics at Barcelona, Spain, are attended by the Unified Team of CIS

1993–A majority of the CIS states agree to disband the supreme command of the CIS joint armed forces, in transition to coordinated CIS forces, which leaves unresolved tense issues such as ownership of the Black Sea fleet and control of still existing strategic nuclear weapons deployed amongst several states; indications are that Russia, which supplies major energy to several states, is using energy and cutting supplies as a weapon in settling ethnic disputes such as local citizenship laws; Russia's military is supposed to play peacekeeper in ethnic and political feuds across the former Soviet Union but there is evidence that Russia is playing favorites; some states resent Russia's dominant political and economic force in the region and are searching for sources of energy within their own borders or contracting with foreign countries; the IMF announces development of a new program of loans for the CIS designed to boost the import-export factor by upgrading the industrial sectors; political extremists revolting against economic and political problems disrupt the May Day parade causing hundreds to be injured in the worst political violence since the 1991 coup against Gorbachev

1994—The Kazakhstan Parliament votes to move its capital from Almaty (formerly Alma-Ata) to Akmola, a more central location; Russia signs a contract with DeBeers for diamond production in exchange for loans; Russia makes a landmark agreement for cooperation and security by enrolling in NATO's Partnership for Peace program; Russia signs an agreement with the EU setting certain economic terms and quotas that should improve the economy; the agreement also lays out standards for human rights and democracy

IMPORTANT PEOPLE

Chizgiz Aitmatov, Kyrgyz author

Mukhtar Auezov, Kazakh author

Isaak Babel (1894-1941), writer; works include *Red Cavalry and Other Stories*

Aleksandr Borodin (1833-87), composer and chemist; known for the opera *Prince Igor* and the symphonic poem *In the Steppes of Central Asia*

Karl Bryullov, artist

Mikhail Bulgakov (1891-1940), novelist and playwright; novels include *The Master and Margarita*

Anton Chekhov (1860-1904), dramatist and writer; plays include *The Cherry Orchard* and *Uncle Vanya*

Fyodor Dostoyevsky (1821-81), novelist; writings include *Crime and Punishment* and *The Brothers Karamazov*

Sergei Eisenstein (1898-1948), film director best known for his 1925 film *Battleship Potemkin*

Aleksandr Fadeyev (1901-56), novelist

Konstantin A. Fedin (1892-1977), novelist

Ivan Franko, Ukrainian author

Yuri Gagarin (1934-68), cosmonaut; first man to travel in space

Nikolai Gogol (1809-52), novelist; writings include *Dead Souls* and *Inspector General*

Mikhail Gorbachev (1931-   ), last general secretary of the Soviet Communist party

Vladimir Horowitz (1904-89), pianist

Aleksandr Ivanov, artist

Dmitri Kabalevsky, composer

Aram Khachaturian (1903-78), composer of symphonic music and music for the Armenian national anthem

Tikhon Khrenikov, composer

Orest Kiprensky, artist

Mikhail Kotsyubinsky (1864-1913), Ukrainian author

Lenin (Vladimir Ilyich Ulyanov) (1870-1924), revolutionary leader; founder of the Bolshevik party; first Communist leader of the Soviet Union

Leonid M. Leontov, novelist

Mikhail Lermentov (1814-41), romantic poet and novelist

Dmitri Levitsky, artist

Kazimir Malevich (1878-1935), artist

Abdizhamil Murpeisov, Kazakh author

Modest Mussorgsky (1839-81), composer; works include opera *Boris Godunov* and piano compositions such as *Pictures at an Exhibition*

Nicholas II (1868-1918), last tsar of Russia; executed with his family after the 1917 revolution

Boris Pasternak (1890-1960), poet and novelist; won Nobel prize for literature in 1958; writings include *Doctor Zhivago*

Peter I (1672-1725), tsar, called Peter the Great, who brought Russia into the modern world

Arkady Plastov, artist

Sergei Prokofiev (1891-1953), pianist and composer; works include music for Eisenstein's films, piano concertos, ballets, and *Peter and the Wolf* for children young and old

Aleksandr Pushkin (1799-1837), poet

Sergei Rachmaninoff (1873-1943), composer, pianist, and conductor; *Prelude in C-Sharp Minor* is one of his best-known compositions

Ilya Repin (1844-1930), painter

Nicholas Rimsky-Korsakov (1844-1908), composer; remembered for "Flight of the Bumble Bee" from an opera and symphonic suite entitled *Scheherazade*

Mstislav Rostropovich (1927-   ), cellist and conductor

Andrei Rublev, artist

Andrei Dmitriyevich Sakharov (1921-89), physicist and a crusader for human rights; awarded 1975 Nobel Prize for Peace

Svetlana Savitskaya, first woman to walk in space

Valentin Serov, artist

Taras Shevchenko (1814-61), Ukrainian poet; called father of Ukrainian national literature

Mikhail A. Sholokhov (1905-84), novelist; awarded Nobel prize for literature in 1965; writings include *And Quiet Flows the Don*

Dmitri Shostakovich (1906-75), composer; considered greatest symphonist of the mid-twentieth century

Alexandr Solzhenitsyn (1918-   ), writer; won Nobel prize for literature in 1970; writings include *Gulag Archipelago* and *One Day in the Life of Ivan Denisovich*

Joseph Stalin (1879-1953), dictator of the Soviet Union from 1929 to 1953

Igor Stravinsky (1882-1971), considered one of the greatest composers of twentieth century; composed ballets, symphonies, chamber music, songs, and piano pieces

Vasili Surikov, artist

Peter Tchaikovsky (1840-93), composer of operas, ballets such as *Swan Lake*, symphonies, chamber music, piano pieces, the *1812 Overture*, and other works

Nikolai Tikhonov, poet

Leo Tolstoy (1828-1910), novelist and philosopher; writings include *War and Peace* and *Anna Karenina*

Ivan Turgenev (1818-83), novelist, poet, literary critic, and playwright

Mirzo Tursunzade, Tajik poet

Lesya Ukrainka (1871-1913), born Larisa Kosach-Kvitka; Ukrainian poet

Andrei Voznesensky, poet

Mikhail Vrubel, artist

Boris Yeltsin (1931-   ), first president of the Russian republic, and of the CIS

Yevgeni Yevtushenko, poet

Mikhail Zoshchenko (1895-1958), short story writer

INDEX

Page numbers that appear in boldface type indicate illustrations

Interrepublican Economic
  Committee, 29
Irkutsk, 70, **71, 84**
iron ore, 11
Irtysh River, 11-12, 126
Islam, 74-76, 124
Israel, 75
Ivanov, Aleksandr, 100, 135
Jewish population, 51, 75
Jewish religion, 75, 76, 124
Kabalevsky, Dmitri, 102, 135
Kamchatka Peninsula, 13, **13** ,
  110, **110**
Kandinsky, Vasily, 100
Karagiye Depression, 126
Kara-Kum canal, 62, 126
Kazakh people, 22, 58, **58** , 61,
  124, 133
Kazakhstan, 8, **12**, 14, 18, 19, 22,
  57-59, **58**, **59**, 93, 106, 108, 118,
  119, 124, 128, 131
Kazan, 126
Khabarovsk, 70, **70**
Khachaturian, Aram, 102, 135
Kharkov, 48, 125
Khrenikov, Tikhon, 102, 135
Khrushchev, Nikita, 133
Kiev, 10, 47-48, **47**, **48**, **49**, 52,
  125, 128
Kiprensky, Orest, 100, 135
Kirghiz people, 22, 60, 82, 128,
  133
Kirov troupe (ballet), 103
Kishinev, 50, **51**
Komsomol, 85
Kopet Mountains, 62
Kotsyubinsky, Mikhail, 99, 135
Koussevitsky, Serge, 102
Krasnoyarsk, 70, 111, 128, 132
Kremlin, 36, **37**, 38, 101, **101**, 130
Kremlin Palace of Congresses,
  38, 133
Krikalev, Sergei, 119
Kuibyshev, 70, 126. *See also*
  Samara
Kyrgyzstan, 8, 19, 22, 57, 60-61,
  60, 106, 124, 128
lakes, **56**, 71-72, 126
languages, 33, 50, 57, 61, 68, 74,
  88, 125
Latvia, 8, 22, 30, 124, 133, 134

League of Nations, 133
Lena River, 11-12, 126
Lenin, Vladimir, **20**, 21, 132, 136
Leningrad, 40, 51, 134. *See also*
  St. Petersburg
  siege of, 133
Lenin Peak, 67
Lenin's Tomb, 36, **37**, 38, 130
Leontov, Leonid M., 98, 136
Lermentov, Mikhail, 97, 136
Levitsky, Dmitri, 100, 136
literacy rate, 112, 129-130
literature, 61, 92, 95, 96-100, 130
Lithuania, 8, 22, 30, 52, 124, 133,
  134
livestock, 60-61, **60**, **61**, 66, 67,
  108, 138
Lutheran religion, 75
Lutsk, 48
L'viv, 48, 69
Malevich, Kazimir, 100, 136
manufacturing, 107, 128
maps
  geographic sections, **10**
  land regions, **15**
  political, **123**
  regional, **1**
  republics, **8**
markets economy, 30
marriage, 77, 130-131
marshlands, 12
May Day, 90-91, **91**, 130
measures, 135
merchant marine, 115
Milstein, Nathan, 102
mining, 11, 128
Minsk, 51-52, **52**, 124, 125, 131
Mislimov, Shirali, 55
Moldova, 8, 17, 50-51, **50**, **51**,
  106, 124, 128, 134
money, 125
Moscow, **2**, 7, 10, 22, 23, **24**, 33,
  35-39, **35**, **36**, **37**, **38**, **39**, 47, 51,
  73, **101**, 125
Moscow Circus, **103**
Moscow University, 36, **36**, 130
Moskva River, **2**, 35, **36**, **39**
mosques, 57, **65**, 75, 76
mountains, 10-11, 12, **12**, 19, **19**,
  59, 67, **67**, 68, **100**, **120**, 126
mud slides, 59

About the Author

Abraham Resnick, a native New Jerseyan, is a noted author and educator specializing in elementary and secondary social studies education. Recently retired, he served for many years as a professor of education at Jersey City State College.

Dr. Resnick has had an outstanding career writing many student-level and professional books. His titles include an array of subjects, including books about countries of the world, maps and globes, American holidays, the Holocaust, the state of New Jersey, and ideas for teachers. He has received two writing awards from the National Council for Geographic Education as well as numerous honors.

The author enlisted in the armed forces during World War II and served as a weatherman in the United States Army Air Corps.

Abe Resnick has a number of diverse interests. He enjoys cooking, watching sporting events, playing golf, bowling, long-distance walking, travel to remote regions of the world, and playing with his five young grandchildren.

Dr. Resnick also has written *Russia: A History to 1917* and *The Union of Soviet Socialist Republics: A Survey from 1917 to 1991* in the Enchantment of the World series.